LETTERS TO THE FUTURE

An Approach to Sinyavsky-Tertz

By the same author

Sagittarius in Warsaw
Soldier and Tsar in the Forest (translation)

LETTERS TO THE FUTURE

An Approach to Sinyavsky-Tertz

RICHARD LOURIE

Cornell University Press

ITHACA AND LONDON

International Standard Book Number 0-8014-0890-3
Library of Congress Catalog Card Number 74-10413

Printed in the United States of America by Vail-Ballou Press, Inc.

To my parents

Contents

Preface

The first appearance of the works of Abram Tertz in 1959 and the sudden arrest of the teacher and literary critic Andrei Sinyavsky in 1965 for being the author of those works were both events typical of a closed society, and there was nothing remarkable in them apart from the particular genius of Sinyavsky-Tertz. In an open society, a certain portion of whose workings is constantly exposed to public view, events can be observed as they unfold. The importance of a free press in maintaining maximum transparency can hardly be exaggerated. The sudden arrival of a mature talent from obscurity would, in an open society, be due to entirely different causes from those that governed the metamorphosis of Sinyavsky into Tertz. In a closed society processes are nearly invisible, and only end-products, results, accomplished facts can be seen. In that regard Sinyavsky's spiritual rebellion was carried out in the same clandestine manner in which all Soviet society operates.

For Sinyavsky to have openly attempted his quest for a genuine identity and authentic knowledge would have been little short of suicidal. He was compelled to live like a Marrano, except that, instead of practicing his religion in secret, he was discovering it as part of the self, having first to find his way out of a maze of illusions. Nothing was sudden in the process of discovery except the shock of events from without; what was truly remarkable was not only the works themselves but the spiritual travail from which they arose and which united them.

Sinyavsky's evolution not only is reflected in his works but has been, in part, created by them. His use of scepticism, irony, and satire helped him purge himself of lies and dogma, and humor helped him to surmount fear and to keep his balance in the dangerous interlude between the destruction of one faith and the creation of another. By the time of his arrest Sinyavsky had found what he had set out to find—a new and permanent point of balance within himself.

Since literature played more than a purely "literary" role in Sinyavsky's life, I do not limit myself here to cataloguing his devices and themes or to tracking down the influence of other writers on his work. Rather I prefer to treat his writings as visible signs of complex and changing relationships. Though it is necessary to break these relationships down into discrete units for proper understanding—Sinyavsky and Soviet society, Sinyavsky and Russia, Sinyavsky the critic and Tertz the artist, for example—the fact that all were parts of a unified process should not be lost sight of. That process must be termed religious because the impulse behind it was to be satisfied only by the facing and the resolving of the ultimate human problems.

Several times during the writing of this book I asked myself and was asked by others whether the publication of a work on Sinyavsky might not jeopardize his safety. I concluded that it would not; quite the reverse, for an international reputation has served more than one Soviet author in time of need. Happily, the arrival of Sinyavsky in the West has relieved me of that concern. It is my hope that this book will bring Sinyavsky a larger audience who will see that he ranks with Solzhenitsyn as a master of modern Russian fiction.

I would like to thank Kathryn Feuer, Czesław Miłosz, Aleksander Wat, Gleb Struve, and Hugh McLean, who were all, directly or indirectly, of great help to me in this book. I would also like to thank the Humanities Foundation for assisting me in my research on Vasily Rozanov, much of which was incorporated into Chapter 5.

RICHARD LOURIE

LETTERS TO THE FUTURE
An Approach to Sinyavsky-Tertz

I am convinced that most books are letters to the future . . .

Abram Tertz, "The Icicle"

I

The Metamorphosis
of Sinyavsky-Tertz

Andrei Sinyavsky and his metamorphosis into Abram Tertz cannot be understood without a sense of the specific culture that nurtured, shaped, and menaced Sinyavsky. Whether or not Russia is a world unto itself or dramatic proof of the breadth of European civilization is an old and intriguing question which will be looked at, through Sinyavsky's eyes, at the proper time; the problem here, however, is to sketch in the particular milieu of the Soviet intellectual, with its own distinct dimensions of experience and points of reference. Sinyavsky is read in the West not only because he became a celebrated victim and because he takes his readers into formerly blank areas in the Soviet psyche, but also because his literary talent and philosophic independence make him one of the most important and innovative writers in the world today. But it would be a serious error immediately to elevate Sinyavsky to a general, human level and discuss him there; his writings and the example of his fate must be seen first in their native habitat and only then in the zoo of abstractions.

Enough is known about Sinyavsky to form some impression of him as a man, to glimpse his character and the details of his daily life, but there are far too many gaps, and a portrait based on hearsay cannot much resemble its subject. According to the transcript of his trial, one of the items confiscated when Sinyavsky was arrested was a manuscript entitled "An Essay in Self-Analysis" (also known as "Taking a Reading"; its Russian title is "Tochka otcheta"), of whose contents absolutely nothing is known. The knowledge that such an unpublished manuscript exists must necessarily temper any judgment of the man or his works, though there is little likelihood that its contents would radically alter the image formed by his other writings.

Sinyavsky received the degree of "candidate of philological sciences" (roughly a doctorate) from Moscow State University in 1952 after his dissertation on Gorky's unfinished novel, *Klim Samgin*, was accepted. Soon thereafter he became a senior research fellow at the Gorky Institute of World Literature, also in Moscow. It is about the Sinyavsky of these years that we have the most information. Literature was a passion for him, a passion he communicated to his students. One of them, Michel Aucouturier, a young Frenchman who was one of the first foreigners to study in Moscow after Stalin's death in 1953, remembers him this way: "Chain smoking as he spoke warmly and intelligently about Alexander Blok, he created in his small classroom an atmosphere of hushed concentration which was in marked contrast to the boredom which prevailed in the big lecture hall we had till then attended."[1] There was always a stream of students to the Sinyavsky home, a communal apartment, whose kitchen and bath were shared with four other families, and which was located in the old Arbat section of Moscow. The small apartment was decorated with old ikons and speciments of folk art that Sinyavsky and his wife, the former Maya Vasilevna Rozanova-Kruglikova, had brought back from their trips to the north Russian hinterland. (At the time of his arrest Sinyavsky was working on a book entitled "Earth and Heaven," an analysis of the Russian view of life as expressed in ancient works of art, especially ikons.) With few material comforts (of no great importance to them) and in a constant struggle to make ends meet, Sinyavsky and his wife provided their guests with that feast of human qualities—intimacy, cordiality, hospitality, marvelous conversation—familiar to every traveler to Russia who has had the good fortune to spend an evening in the home of Russian intellectuals. Svetlana Alliueva recalls in *Only One Year* [2] how delightful it was just to sit and listen to Sinyavsky's Russian—a point that comes up again in the reminiscence of Sinyavsky's student, J. Bonamour:

He was an admirable storyteller. It was not so much his ideas or even his knowledge that created the deepest impression. To the felicities of a brilliant style, which often detract from the underlying thought, he preferred a homely image or even a parable which struck one at first as a humorous aside, a good-natured way of making fun of things; but, on second thought, one realized that the image, the joke, were a shortcut to understanding the subject, grasping its true significance; after that it would never be forgotten, and would become the starting-point of one's own ideas. [3]

Both as a public and a private person, Sinyavsky was leading a rich, fulfilling, and useful life; his interests ranged from modern art to tales of witchcraft and the supernatural, from French poetry to the songs of criminals, and his career as teacher and critic was progressing nicely, following a more or less liberal line through the tilts and reversals of the Thaw. Some of his readings must have prepared him for his metamorphosis into Tertz, though it would be most unwise to seek the roots of his metamorphosis in books alone. As a senior research fellow, Sinyavsky had access to books unavailable to the average reader. Many Russian works that are on the Soviet Index nevertheless circulate in old, prerevolutionary editions, and much modern European and American literature finds its way into the Soviet Union. There are conflicting reports about the unofficial half of Sinyavsky's education. One former student of his, Claude Frioux, remarks, speaking of Sinyavsky and Daniel together:

Both were men of deep and wide culture, a culture which had none of the surprising gaps displayed, inevitably in those days, by even the most attractive Soviet intellectuals. . . . They knew almost all that mattered about twentieth-century Western literature . . . and had read all the works of the Romantic-Revolutionary school of the twenties, which the Stalinists had done their utmost to destroy.[4]

On the other hand, Hélène Zamoyska, who knew Sinyavsky well and was his courier for getting his manuscripts out of the Soviet Union, says:

"There were, of course, inevitable gaps in his knowledge

—he had not read Kafka or Pirandello, nor Proust or Joyce." [5] If such gaps did exist, they would only prove that a man can become a first-rate writer without having read the masters of European modernity. This would seem especially true for a Russian writer with different experiences and traditions to draw upon; after all, personal knowledge of Stalin's Russia would lessen Kafka's novelty somewhat, and the memories that the Russians in the late fifties and early sixties had to confront were very different from those of Marcel Proust. From Zamoyska we know that Sinyavsky had a very strong attachment to French literature and learned the language in order to read in the original such writers as Villon, Baudelaire, Rimbaud, Blaise Cendrars, Malraux, and Celine; and he was also much taken with Whitman and Verhaeren. In addition, Sinyavsky was the coauthor of a book on Picasso. It must be said that he had his windows to the West and was shaped to some degree by that exposure. But neither the style nor the substance of his writings can be traced directly to those Western influences, nor can his decision to assume a double life.

Very few traces of influence of this sort can be found in Sinyavsky's writings, and his attitude toward the West has been anything but uncritical; admiration, scorn, jealousy, and metaphysical suspicions are all mixed together in it according to an old Russian recipe. Aucouturier relates that Russia and the West were Sinyavsky's favorite themes in conversation and quotes him as saying:

"You think that your freedom, your culture, your parliaments can become ideals to us? To us? We who made the revolution, who have believed in Communism, who have shed our blood so that justice and freedom should reign over the world forever!" [6]

Both Westerners and Soviet bureaucrats are guilty of exaggerating the seductive power of European culture and ideals over Russian intellectuals. Sinyavsky's allegiances, at a given moment, were to Russia, Russian literature and to the ideals of the Revolution, but these were by no means the simple allegiances that warm the hearts of rulers.

In Russia more than in most countries, literature is part of life and history: it is the collective reflecting on itself in motion, at once conscience and consciousness. Sinyavsky's tastes, to some degree typical of those of the contemporary literary intelligentsia, are more than just a matter of individual preference, for they include as well his sense of his own place in a social continuum. For more than twenty years, from the early thirties to the death of Stalin, Russian literature was dominated by the officially created and officially enforced doctrine of Socialist Realism, whose results have been brilliantly analyzed by Sinyavsky in *On Socialist Realism*. Since the principal feature of this period was the virtual destruction of the Russian literary tradition, the more perceptive writers of the fifties understood the healing of that sundered tradition to be one of their prime responsibilities. Solzhenitsyn, for example, returns to the sceptical translucent mode of Chekhov and Tolstoy, whereas Sinyavsky, whose literary background is more varied than Solzhenitsyn's, connects himself up with a series of traditions. Sinyavsky finds his stylistic ancestors in Gogol, Remizov,

Bely, and Leskov, who wrote so-called ornamental prose in which the texture of language is as integral a part of the narrative as the movement of events or the delineation of character is. In some cases, this texturing of language becomes the event and the means of character delineation. Most of Sinyavsky's contemporaries, Nagibin, Kazakov, and others, have aligned themselves with the tradition of Russian realism in which there is no attempt to draw any attention to the devices of narration in order to better sustain the illusion of actual events. And those writers of the Thaw who saw their task as the exploration of the subtle nuances of personal life, so neglected in the era of Socialist Realism, were naturally attracted to the Chekhovian mode of simplicity, understatement, the telling detail. Solzhenitsyn's use of a somewhat old-fashioned realism may have more than a single source; he is much less a literary man than Sinyavsky is. Perhaps the overwhelming nature of Solzhenitsyn's personal experiences (the war, labor camps, cancer) has kept him from achieving the sort of aesthetic distance that Sinyavsky was able to fashion for himself in his quiet, contemplative years at the Gorky Institute. Perhaps Solzhenitsyn's moral passion for justice dictated his choice of form, in the belief that semidocumentary realism raised to the level of art was the best means of remaining true to the letter and spirit of the age.

Sinyavsky based his experiments with form on the literature of the twenties, the last brilliant flare before the lights went out. This literature is doubly dear to him: it is daringly experimental, and it is associated in his mind with the romantic phase of the Revolution, its early struggles and heroic days which, though they were bloody (or because they were) had for him at one time an almost mystic authority. The last writings of Blok, the poetry of Tsvetaeva, Mandelstam, Zabolotsky, Akhmatova, Pasternak, and Mayakovsky, the prose of Babel, Olesha, and Zoshchenko attracted Sinyavsky as a corpus of outstanding works. He found points of contact with each writer and has written about most of them. It would seem that a break in tradition such as that suffered by Russian literature would be more damaging to poetry than to prose, though, fortunately, history does not contain enough such instances to make any worthwhile analogies. But poetry does grow by minute accretions, and gaps can be disastrous; much of the Russian poetry of the fifties and early sixties seems dated because the poets of those decades had to return to the severed ends of the earlier tradition and carefully weave a connection between them and the present age. Sinyavsky's own style, with its ellipses and musical structures, owes a great deal to his close readings of twentieth-century Russian poets, and as a teacher and critic he helped cultivate an atmosphere in which their poetry could be understood, appreciated, and accepted.

Sinyavsky's cast of mind, its categories and habits, are products of a Soviet education in the largest possible sense of the word, but there is more to his intellectual makeup than dialectical thought patterns; there is also the legacy of the metaphysical quest associated with the Symbolist poets and philosophers of the Silver Age who arose in the twenty

years preceding the Revolution. Dostoevsky, their progeni-
tor, was the prophet of the idea that individual life is
essentially a religious passion, not a social phenomenon; his
direct successors include Solovev, Rozanov, and Berdyaev,
who in his study of Dostoevsky's world-view claimed the
two greatest influences on his own life were Jesus Christ
and Dostoevsky.[7] The Symbolist movement was in part a
reaction to the social imperatives of Russian literature and
thought, and in part a realization of the lateness of the
hour, of the inevitability of social upheaval. But for a
Soviet intellectual such metaphysical concerns are no more
proper than were erotic extravaganzas for a New England
Puritan; they were relegated to the nether world of Sinyavsky's mind, where heretical thoughts, bizarre fantasies,
the itch for creative experiment, and personal obsessions
gathered and fermented. Realizing that he could not safely
deal with the contents of his imagination publicly through
literature, Sinyavsky decided to treat his imagination as a
quasi-separate personality to which he gave the name
"Abram Tertz." As Tertz he would taste the joys and bear
the burdens of creative freedom or "inner freedom," as it
is called by the dissidents. But it would be an anxious and
uneasy freedom, for, from the beginning, Sinyavsky knew
that it was only a matter of time until he was discovered.

There were outside forces at work in the creation of
Tertz. Like all Soviet citizens, Sinyavsky lived in an atmosphere directly influenced by political and historical events
—the purges of the thirties, the war, the final years of
Stalinism, the denunciation of Stalin at the Twentieth Party

Congress, the hopes of the Khrushchev era—and like many Soviet citizens he was to become personally and tragically involved in the course of events.

On February 10, 1966, the first day of his trial, Sinyavsky was described in the indictment as follows:

Sinyavsky, Andrei Donatovich, born October 8, 1925, Russian, not a member of the Party, native of Moscow, father of a young son, member of the Union of Soviet Writers, senior research fellow at the Institute of World Literature of the Academy of Sciences of the USSR, resident of Moscow.[8]

Subsequent testimony revealed that Sinyavsky's father had been arrested in 1951 and that Sinyavsky had served in the army toward the end of the war, but apparently without seeing any combat. He was a *Komsomolets* (member of the Young Communist League) from 1947 to 1950. We also know that he began his clandestine writing career as Abram Tertz in 1956 and that he and Yuli Daniel (his codefendant) served as pallbearers at Boris Pasternak's funeral in 1960. That is practically all the factual knowledge available about Sinyavsky, and yet even from these flat statistics a great drama may be inferred.

The date and place of his birth and the place of his residence are significant. Born in 1925, Sinyavsky is a true child of the Soviet era; for him the Revolution and the Civil War are not memories but myths, stories told him by his father, and we have already seen in his outburst against Western ideals the strength of his feelings for the Revolution's early years and its ideals. Growing up in the capital, serving in the army but without seeing action, and then, in the post-

war years attending Moscow University, where by his
natural talents and intelligence he quickly distinguished
himself, Sinyavsky was progressing smoothly in a life somewhat special and sheltered by Russian standards. Membership in the Komsomol is essential for upward mobility and
thus need not indicate any ideological commitment, but
there is no reason to think that for Sinyavsky it was anything but a normal move based on his fervor and his standing in society. Zamoyska, whose friendship with him began
in 1947, describes the Sinyavsky of that time:

Sinyavsky, the son of an active revolutionary, shared his family's
cult of the Revolution and their contempt for army officers as
a class; he belonged to the Communist League of Youth and
was, needless to say, an atheist. . . . Sinyavsky was a completely convinced Communist. There were many reasons for
this: The word "Revolution" had for him the same emotional
overtones as "liberté" has for Frenchmen. The heroes who
fired his imagination—Zhelyabov, Sofia Perovskaya, Dzerzhin-
sky—had been devoted to it heart and soul. . . . If Sinyavsky
so admired Communism, it was largely because it had given
birth to this fanatical race of dedicated men and women who
lived up to their convictions at the cost of everything they
held most dear. . . . Yet his attitude was not merely emotional.
He was deeply marked by his intellectual training. Marxism
offered a complete view of life and thus a rational basis for his
need of the absolute and of social justice. What attracted him
was not so much the logic of its allegedly scientific laws as the
dialectical method as such, the flexibility of mind it favored,
and above all the Marxist philosophy of history. Truth was historical and Communism embodied it in our time. Wasn't this
sufficiently proved by the Soviet Union's achievements in the

war and by her place as a world power? Because it appealed to his patriotism this was perhaps the argument which influenced him most.[9]

During the fifties Sinyavsky's father was arrested (1951), Stalin died (1953), Khrushchev denounced Stalin (1956), and Sinyavsky began to produce writings he knew had no chance of being published in the Soviet Union (1956).

If the image that emerges from the accounts of Sinyavsky written by friends and former students has any validity, there can be little doubt that during the years 1950–1956 he underwent a great change. The works he wrote under the pen name of Abram Tertz are a further and conscious development of that change, that new relationship with himself and his society. In many ways Sinyavsky was typical of the younger Soviet intelligentsia, born after the Revolution and raised entirely under the Soviet system, all of whom experienced a great shock in the fifties and passed through a period of reappraisal. But Sinyavsky's abundance of passion and intelligence served to intensify the crisis he passed through so that the form it took was exceptionally dramatic, the creation of the Sinyavsky-Tertz relationship. But even this itself is not without parallel if one recalls Daniel-Arzhak, though for Daniel, one feels, neither the conflict not the talent was as great as Sinyavsky's.

To reduce a significant transformation to a simple formula, on the order of "Loyal Komsomolets becomes underground rebel," would be to neglect the tangle of crossed loyalties that gives Sinyavsky's struggles their special richness and complexity. Personalities seem always to retain their basic contradictions in one form or another. One may suspect that Sinyavsky the Komsomolets had his doubts (though we certainly have enough accounts of the internal mechanisms by which such doubts are rationalized) and that, after his sentencing, Sinyavsky had his regrets (because it is only human to regret parting with a young son for seven years). Nevertheless, all the respect owed to complexity should not be allowed to obscure the dimensions of the change undergone by Sinyavsky.

Accounts of Sinyavsky in the late forties all indicate that his loyalty to the Revolution and its ideals, heroes, and martyrs was in no way as yet separated from a loyalty to the existing regime. His eventual change represented in essence a splitting of this loyalty which, in turn, necessitated a reorganization of his values. By 1956 this split had become acute and conscious, and it may be clearly viewed in his writings of that year, *On Socialist Realism* and *The Trial Begins*. Though there certainly must have been factors at work in Sinyavsky's life prior to 1950 to prepare him for the changes wrought by and in the years 1950–1956, it is to those years that we must look for the heightening and quickening of that division of values.

For Sinyavsky the crucial events of the first six years of the fifties were the arrest of his father in 1951, the "Doctors' Plot" of 1952–1953, the death of Stalin in 1953, and Khrushchev's denunciation of Stalin in 1956. His friendship with Boris Pasternak began in 1956, and also his literary career as Abram Tertz. Practically nothing is known of Sinyavsky's father, and Hélène Zamoyska's description of him raises as many questions as it answers. What, for example, were his political affiliations before the Revolution? How did he feel about the Revolution that came to pass? Had he ever been arrested before?

Sinyavsky's father had been active in the non-Bolshevik revolutionary movements before 1917. Later, he took part as a volunteer in the collectivisation of the land and narrowly escaped death at the hands of villagers who obviously had not been convinced by his arguments. This made a great impression on Sinyavsky. The dangerous life his father had lived endowed the ideals he fought for with an aura of romanticism and made the Revolution, and the social order it led to, sacred for Andrey.[10]

From another source close to Sinyavsky (Alfreda Aucouturier) we have more details about the arrest of his father, at which Sinyavsky was present: "His arrest at two o'clock in the morning was followed by a house-search that went on for forty-eight hours." [11] Fourteen years later, at his own trial, Sinyavsky himself recalled at "during the search one of the MGB people had said that I ought to be arrested together with my father." [12]

This remark by the MGB man, which must have struck Sinyavsky with enormous force, was in fact a gratuitous detail of fate. Sinyavsky's own conscience would have suggested the same sentiment sooner or later. If his father was, as Zamoyska suggests, a symbol of revolutionary faith to Sinyavsky and a link to the heroic events of the past, the arrest must have shocked not only Sinyavsky's feelings but his faith as well, and it could have seemed to him a symbolic

arrest of the Revolution by those in power, who had
betrayed its ideals. Though it is dangerous to connect
biography and fiction, the following quote from *The Trial
Begins* can hardly be viewed as pure invention:

> The doorbell rings. Surname? Christian name? Date of birth?
> This is when you begin to write.[13]

In fact, the motif of the writer fearing imminent arrest runs
throughout Sinyavsky's work and provides one of the few
ominous notes in his last novel, *The Makepeace Experiment*,
otherwise marked by a Pushkinian lightness of creative
spirit. Sinyavsky's father was one of the many who returned as a result of the amnesties granted by the Twentieth
Party Congress in 1956, and he died shortly thereafter.

The so-called Doctors' Plot, which must have had special
significance for Sinyavsky, coming as it did so soon after
the arrest of his father, serves as the background of his
first novel, *The Trial Begins*. Stalin's death (which also
figures in *The Trial Begins*) and Khrushchev's denunciation of him had enormous impact on Soviet society, and the
ramifications of these events are still being felt. The denunciation created a division between regime and Revolution, a break in continuity with the original events and personalities, and such continuity is especially important in a
form of government in which succession has an ideological
basis. Since 1956 the great efforts that have been made to
stress the essential continuity of the Soviet government
have necessitated another reappraisal of Stalin, once again
stressing his positive contributions. Nevertheless, the dam-

age was essentially irreparable. (As Sinyavsky remarks in *On Socialist Realism*, teleological systems must never be seen in a compromising light.) It had become possible to think of the regime and the Revolution as divisible concepts, with a corresponding split in loyalties also becoming feasible. The Thaw created an atmosphere of relatively free inquiry, of individual and collective soul-searching, of renewed resolve and rededicated loyalty, but a loyalty that was, for many, never again to be unquestioning, uncritical, or indivisible. Sinyavsky described to Zamoyska his own reaction to the Khrushchev denunciations: "I know how much the Soviet Union means to me by the depth of my shame when I heard the report." [14]

He told Michel Aucouturier that, for him, "de-Stalinization meant above all a return to the creative vigour unleashed by the Revolution." [15]

These remarks are testimony to Sinyavsky's abiding faith in the myth of the Revolution. His stance, in other words, is not anti-Soviet and is similar to that taken by many intellectuals whose faith was shaken but not destroyed. Though the crimes against "Socialist legality" detailed by Khrushchev in his "secret" denunciation speech were common knowledge to many Russians (who, like Sinyavsky, had felt the criminal hand of Stalin in their own lives), few people were aware of their scope. By acknowledging the crimes the leadership not only confirmed suspicions but "legitimatized" them, a key factor in the Soviet Union where reality is defined from above.

Another stage in the metamorphosis of Sinyavsky into

Tertz concerns Russian literature in general and Boris Pasternak in particular. The essential character of Russian literature is clearly delineated by Czesław Miłosz, the Polish poet and essayist, in his introduction to the first American edition of *On Socialist Realism:*

Literature in Western Europe and America has never had the social character it possesses in Eastern Europe, except perhaps during the Reformation, when the writer spoke on behalf of a specific religious community. Although the political part played by certain writers has sometimes been great (Rousseau and Voltaire are obvious instances) the collective imagination has never had its archetype of bard, leader, and teacher.[16]

The archetype of the poet may be eternal, but the specific situation in which it operates does much to either vitalize or vitiate its power. During the late eighteenth century in Russia, the poet and the state began to assume mutually hostile positions. (Catherine the Great was expressing this hostility when she called Radishchev "worse than Pugachev.") The rulers of Russia have always depended on a mystique backed up by force, and although they have almost always been confident of their superior force, their natural enemy has been the bearer of consciousness, the Promethean poet, who challenges the mystique and consequently the rulers and the regime. In Russia that situation has remained essentially unchanged from the time of Catherine II to the present. The archetype of the poet retains much of its primal strength for the only power great enough to diminish its force is democracy, and intellectual democracy does not yet exist in the Soviet Union. Only when the state can be identified as the source of injustice and has forbidden free and open discussion to its citizens, is there sufficient pressure on the collective imagination to galvanize the poet archetype. Of course, if sufficient force is exerted, as it was in Stalin's time, against the poets, they will vanish, returning to a dormant state, as does the archetype of the great warrior in a time of prolonged peace, to reappear as soon as it is necessary or possible.

For many Russians in the decade of the fifties Boris Pasternak was an embodiment of the poet-archetype.[17] He exercised tremendous moral and literary authority, and young poets would often begin their careers by sending their poems to Pasternak for him to pass judgment on them. Moreover, because Pasternak was linked by his life and his work to the twenties, the last period in which there had been any genuine Russian literature, he in a sense embodied the tradition of Russian literature as well as the archetype of the poet. The ties between Sinyavsky and Pasternak were especially close, and there can be little doubt that Pasternak's example was instrumental in Sinyavsky's decision to send his manuscripts abroad as Pasternak had done in the case of *Doctor Zhivago*. Zamoyska writes about Sinyavsky's discovery of Pasternak:

But in 1956 [Sinyavsky] came across the poems from *Zhivago*. They were a revelation to him. To read about Eve, Christ, Mary Magdalen, in a familiar, modern Russian idiom which yet somehow preserved the richness and flavor of the language of the Bible, and to discover that a modern poet living in the Soviet Union could be so inspired by Christianity! [18]

Zamoyska goes on to relate that she met Pasternak in 1956 and that he gave her a copy of *Doctor Zhivago*, which she passed on to Sinyavsky, who "disagreed violently with some of his ideas about Christianity and the role of the personality in history, . . . thought the book badly constructed and some passages too long but . . . was swept away by its warmth, power, vitality, its tone of voice, its 'immense and ineffaceable portrait of Russia.' " [19]

She also reports that in 1956 or 1957, Sinyavsky went to see Pasternak at Peredelkino and was "even more impressed by him as a person than as a writer." [20] For Sinyavsky this time must have been one of extraordinary stress and intensity; besides getting to know Pasternak in 1956, he learned of the full sweep of Stalin's crimes and began his own career as Abram Tertz, all within the space of a year. Four years later he and Yuli Daniel were to be the pallbearers at Pasternak's funeral, an act of personal courage and symbolic defiance because Pasternak had become the object of official ostracism. Sinyavsky may have seen Pasternak's death as the breaking of an important link to the past, and it was an increased sense of the burdens and responsibilities of Russian literature, as well as Pasternak's coffin, that he took on his shoulders that day. At that moment the horizon was empty, for the publication of Solzhenitsyn's *One Day in the Life of Ivan Denisovich* was still two years away.

Though Sinyavsky can be considered a successor to Pasternak, there is a great difference in the two men, a difference that comes out quite clearly in Sinyavsky's introduction to the 1965 edition of Pasternak's poetry. Sinyavsky remained critical of much of Pasternak's thinking and always found him a little too much outside of history: "Pasternak's description of history seems that of someone who is outside it, which is not the case with his description of nature." [21] By 1963, however, Sinyavsky himself in his aphorisms (*Thought Unaware*) was endeavoring to find vantage points outside history or, more precisely, outside an exclusively historical view of life. Apart from any disagreements, Sinyavsky saw Pasternak as a moral witness, a poet of great courage, talent, and integrity, and an example whose implications could not be ignored.

It can be said that there were two great ideals in Sinyavsky's life—the Revolution, symbolized by his father, and Russian literature, embodied in Pasternak. The arrest of his father and the open hostility of the regime to Pasternak were symbolically charged events that took on inner meaning for Sinyavsky and became elements in his crisis. Sinyavsky's hierarchy of values was shattered, but many of the values themselves remained and were reordered, reconstellated. Sinyavsky the teacher, critic, and spokesman for liberalization continued as before, but now he was accompanied by Tertz, the creative innovator and metaphysical seeker, and worked in close cooperation with him.

Sinyavsky realized that he had no chance of publishing his experimental prose in the Soviet Union and that he could not publish abroad under his own name, for, unlike Pasternak, he had no international reputation to protect him. Objective circumstance as well as inner need dictated the choice of a new identity.

The bridge to this new life was his pseudonym Abram Tertz. The choice of this name came up at the trial, and Sinyavsky of course did not admit that he knew of the thieves' song "Abrashka Tertz from Odessa." Since he was a known admirer of such sub-literature, the coincidence, in this case, seems striking, to say the least. Perhaps he chose the name because of its association with Babel's romantic criminals from Odessa, perhaps because it was related to the South (a symbol of the unconscious, which Sinyavsky was about to explore), perhaps its Jewish flavor attracted him because he was to touch on many of the sore spots in the relationship between Russians and Russian Jews (with a hint of identification with the victim, for the Doctors' Plot was still fresh in his mind), or perhaps the purely criminal aspect of it attracted him because he knew that by beginning his new career he had become a criminal in the eyes of the state. That he had become a criminal by remaining loyal to the highest ideals of Russian literature and the Revolution was just the sort of irony Sinyavsky-Tertz would enjoy. And there was a trace of guilt in the whole process, a contradictory guilt—that he hadn't been arrested with his father and thus wasn't worthy of the Revolution, and that he was at the same time betraying the Revolution, which had been associated in his mind with the regime and Russia for so long that he was never able to see them as utterly separate entities.

At the end of *The Trial Begins* the narrator and "author" of the work says:

I was accused of slander, pornography, and giving away State secrets. . . . In the course of the investigation it was established that everything I had written was pure invention, the product of a morbid and ill-intentioned mind.[22]

As many commentators have pointed out, this fictional trial contains an almost clairvoyant description of the actual charges and workings of Sinyavsky's own trial some ten years later. The similarity of fact and fiction can be attributed to his insights into the workings of post-Stalinist Russia with its fetish of legal formalities, and to his knowledge of the show trials of the thirties. But there is another element. *The Trial Begins* was written in 1956, and we have already seen what a crucial year that was for Sinyavsky. In the novel's epilogue the narrator states: "I had come to the camp later than the others, in the summer of '56." [23] This means that Sinyavsky's first work of fiction, written in 1956, has its "author" being arrested in the same year.

From the very outset, Sinyavsky knew that his clandestine career involved a high probability, if not the certainty, of being discovered and punished. He was even aware of the charges that would be brought against him. Under the pressure of events, both private and public, his personality had broken into Tertz and Sinyavsky, but that split was intended to be a temporary compromise with a hostile reality, to buy time for Sinyavsky to remake himself. Zamoyska shares this opinion:

The possibility of writing without constraint taught him that freedom of conscience and speech were not an anarchistic, individualistic luxury dangerous to the common good (as he had formerly thought under the influence of his education), but a fundamental human necessity and the condition for all progress, individual and social.

For the precious blessing of being entirely himself, he had to risk everything, even seven years in a concentration camp. He expected to be arrested and often spoke to me of it. I am convinced that he desired it, for Abram Tertz had to die. It was only a temporary prop that one day had to be dispensed with when he had acquired enough inner strength to be himself in the eyes of the world and in the ordeal of the trial and the camp.[24]

Sinyavsky was the willing agent of his own fate, which he saw as the price of becoming fully human. His trial and punishment were not only a defeat but a victory, for they marked his fulfillment as a man and an actor in the drama of Russian life, and completed his initiation as a Russian writer.

2

The Trial

The trial of Andrei Sinyavsky and Yuli Daniel, an event at which amorphous historical forces were suddenly arranged into symbolic patterns, is a microcosm of Soviet society at a definite moment in time. In the prelude to the trial and in its actual machinations, as well as in the very principle behind it—that of trying writers for "criminal" ideas—the legacy of the Stalinist past is clear. But new elements are present and old ones absent: the accused did not vanish in the night, they were given the semblance of a trial, and their sentence was not ten to twenty-five years at hard labor or death; moreover, the defendants refused to plead guilty and even went so far as to use the courtroom as a platform for their ideas on cultural freedom; though the trial was held behind closed doors, the young dissident Alexander Ginzburg,[1] managed to attend, transcribe the proceedings, and have that transcript smuggled out of the country to the West, where its contents became known in a very short time. A sense of a fluid situation emerges here, for absolute secrecy and absolute punishment are both absent, and in the government's handling of the situation one detects no singleness of purpose, but rather a response born of compromise and uncertainty, of an allegiance split between the need to punish and the need to save face. On the other hand, the fact that the minutes of the trial were transcribed and smuggled out of the country would seem to indicate that the dissident community not only refused to be intimidated, but was further enraged by the affair.

Sinyavsky's trial has been especially well documented by Louis Labedz and Max Hayward in their book *On Trial*,[2] which contains the minutes, a report on the press campaign against the two writers, and a great deal of other relevant material. The minutes of the trial are a historical document of the first magnitude, indispensable to anyone wishing to understand the relations between politics and culture in the Soviet Union in the mid sixties.

Both Sinyavsky and Daniel, the author of *Moscow Speaking* and several short stories, were arrested in September 1965. On November 22, 1965, at a press conference in Paris, Surkov, the secretary of the Union of Soviet Writers, disclosed that the two writers had been arrested and assured the press they would be guaranteed all legalities in their treatment. The Soviet public received official confirmation of what till then had been only rumor on January 13, 1966, when *Izvestiya* published an article, "The Turncoats," by Dmitri Yeremin. Neither the article's title nor its brutal clichés leave any doubt as to its stance and purpose:

Into what a bottomless quagmire of abomination must a so-called man of letters sink for his hooligan pen to cast a slur upon the name we hold sacred! It is impossible to reproduce here the relevant quotations, so malicious is this drivel, so disgraceful and filthy. By these blasphemous lines alone, the authors have put themselves beyond the pale of Soviet society.[3]

This entire paragraph is a discussion of the attitudes of Sinyavsky and Daniel toward Lenin, and although its prose leaves something to be desired, its structure is highly interesting because it represents the official public response and also because it reveals certain habits of mind. It is, in effect, a syllogism, though its structure is more "dialectical" than logical, a syllogism of indictment proceeding from certain assumed emotional attitudes and articles of faith. The question of guilt or innocence is not left open by Yeremin, who, rather like a medieval theologian measuring Lucifer's fall from heaven in cubits, is interested only in measuring the distance that Sinyavsky and Daniel have fallen, the distance from the heights ("the name we hold sacred") to the depths (a Soviet jail). Having violated the essential legal principle of not prejudging a court case in the press, Yeremin goes on to support his verdict with evidence. In the best tradition of Russian fairy tales, the magnitude of a quality, here guilt, is expressed by terming it inexpressible. The evidence against the two writers is so unbelievably damning because it cannot even be printed in a decent Soviet newspaper. The conclusion can only be that criminals of this sort, by the depth of their fall and by the mass of unprintable evidence, have already put themselves outside the bounds of Soviet society and, by implication, do not even deserve the protection and procedures of the law. Any sentence short of death will be merciful and will reflect the humanity of the state and of Soviet justice.

But Yeremin is not satisfied with turning Sinyavsky and Daniel into blasphemous angels fallen from paradise; fallen angels become devils and labor ceaselessly for the destruction of the good:

They are not just moral perverts but active helpers of those who are stoking up the furnaces of international tension, who would like to turn the cold war into a hot war, and who still nurture the crazy dream of raising their hand against the Soviet Union.[4]

The reader is shown that Sinyavsky and Daniel are their enemies, bent on their destruction, and must be treated in the same manner as spies and saboteurs. Yeremin concludes: "Such helpers can be shown no clemency. Our people have paid too dearly for the gains of October, for the victory over fascism, for the blood and sweat shed on behalf of our homeland, to be indifferent towards these dregs."[5] The allusions to war, fascism, and blood, coupled with October and homeland, are calculated to inflame the patriotic passions of the public, just as the last phrase excuses them from any qualms they might have about impartiality, here called "indifference."

The line taken in this article was picked up and developed in a more literary fashion by Z. Kedrina in her attack on Sinyavsky and Daniel, "The Heirs of Smerdyakov," [6] published in *Literaturnaya gazeta* on January 22, 1966; the moral character of the defendants is again fixed in advance by the title, which relates them to Fyodor Karamazov's bastard son and murderer. Both the press campaign of vilification and the rigged trial were instruments of official policy, and one must wonder why the government chose them when it had other alternatives. After all, the press campaign was hardly necessary and was something of a tactical blunder since its approach carried the stigma of the past and thus signaled the public that an official injustice was to be perpetrated. There are various ways of punishing writers (expulsion from the Writer's Union, black-listing, and so forth) that would have obviated the necessity of a trial and avoided its aftermath—an uproar in the West, damaging to both the international prestige of the Soviet Union and that of foreign communist parties.

To answer any such questions one must look at both the general situation and the particular case of the two writers, remembering always that the answers will be, for the most part, educated guesses. Khrushchev fell from power on October 14, 1964, and in mid November Brezhnev and Kosygin were given the key positions as the Soviet government returned to the principle of collective leadership. The policy that they initiated has been described as both hard and soft (soft in the area of economics, meaning more concern for the Soviet consumer, and hard in the area of armaments, meaning continued expansion and development of Soviet armed might). A campaign by the new government to stress the positive achievement of Stalin was especially prominent in the spring of 1966, more or less coinciding with the time of Sinyavsky's trial. These efforts at Stalin's "rehabilitation" were intended to serve as a corrective to Khrushchev's denunciation of him in 1956, which had weakened the basis of socialist continuity and legitimacy, and caused turmoil in the socialist camp. The new regime has never had any intention of returning to Stalinism: there isn't a Stalin among them, every one has too much to lose from such an about-face, and it is questionable whether Stalinism is the correct approach in a society that has passed through the phase of industrialization and has become increasingly dependent on a new class of technological specialists. But Stalinist methods can be updated and muted. In fact, though the new regime has been cautious and business-like, preferring diplomacy and a "soft" image, it is still committed to the use of severe repressive measures. Sinyavsky and Daniel must have seemed to the successors of Khrushchev another legacy of his era of indiscretion which required terminating. The trial should be viewed in this context, as a signal from above. The behavior of these writers was not to be tolerated. Even if they hadn't done anything specifically illegal, Sinyavsky and Daniel were heretics, not because they had rejected fundamental dogmas, but because they were learning to think in an undogmatic fashion. In effect, the arrest and trial of the two men is a small-scale equivalent of the invasion of Czechoslovakia.

The most important thing to remember is that Daniel and Sinyavsky were not guilty of anything at all. Sending manuscripts outside of the Soviet Union was not a criminal offense, and the charge of slander required that intent be proved, which, in this case, would have been impossible to do in a Western court and was the merest trifle in a Soviet court. The lack of a real crime and the need to punish explain, in part, the stridency of the press campaign. Sinyavsky and Daniel were charged with violations of Section

1 of Article 70 of the Criminal Code of the Russian Republic, which reads:

Agitation or propaganda carried out with the purpose of subverting or weakening the Soviet regime or in order to commit particularly dangerous crimes against the state, the dissemination for the said purposes of slanderous inventions defamatory to the Soviet political or social system, as well as the dissemination or production or harboring for the said purposes of literature of similar context, are punishable by imprisonment for a period of from six months to seven years and with exile from two to five years, or without exile, or by exile from two to five years.

Since the literature in question was fiction and not discursive prose, it was necessary for the court to determine the authors' guilt on the basis of an interpretive reading of their works, in other words, to use literary criticism as an instrument of the prosecution. However, literary criticism is by nature subjective, and a short story cannot be used as evidence in the unambiguous way that fingerprints or bloodstains can. Given the loose wording of Section 1, Article 70, the court could easily enough interpret the works as anti-Soviet and punish the defendants on that basis. As Max Hayward remarks in his introduction to *On Trial*, the trial was unique:

It was the first time in the history of the Soviet Union that writers had been put on trial *for what they had written.* Many Soviet writers have been imprisoned, banished, executed or driven into silence, but never after a trial in which the principal evidence against them was their literary work.[7]

The prosecution sought to attribute the words spoken by certain characters to the authors themselves, an approach based on a purposeful disregard of the nature of literature. It did not matter at all that Sinyavsky demonstrated that other passages could prove his patriotism, or that the works of Gorky and Sholokhov, classics of Soviet literature, contained passages which, if attributed to their authors, would make counterrevolutionaries of them. Sinyavsky gave very little ground and defended his principles well in the face of an implacable court and a foregone verdict; since his own testimony was essentially beside the point, Sinyavsky could have chosen to refuse participation in the court proceedings, for he would have been justified in saying the words later spoken by the dissident author Andrei Amalrik:

Both as a human being who needs creative freedom and a citizen of a country signatory to the Universal Declaration of Human Rights, I consider that this court has no right to try me and I therefore shall not enter into any discussion with the court of my views, shall not give any testimony, and shall not answer any questions put by the court. I do not consider myself guilty of disseminating "lies and slanderous concoctions" and shall not argue here for my innocence, inasmuch as the very principle of freedom of speech rules out the question of my guilt.[8]

The essential absurdity of the trial and its travesty of law is pointed out by Leopold Labedz, who noticed that the judge both accused Sinyavsky of criminal slander for writing that the secret police used bugging devices, and admitted as evidence the tape-recorded conversation obtained by bugging Sinyavsky's apartment. None of this was lost an Sinyavsky, who pointed out the Tertzian quality of the trial:

It is always the same hair-raising quotations from the indictment, repeated dozens of times and mounting up to create a monstrous atmosphere that no longer bears any relation to any kind of reality. It is an artistic device to keep on repeating the same phrases over and over again, and it is a powerful one. It creates a kind of shroud, a peculiar kind of electrified atmosphere in which the boundary between the real and the grotesque becomes blurred, rather as in the works of Arzhak and Tertz.[9]

The trial lasted four days, and both men were found guilty as charged. Sinyavsky received the maximum sentence of seven years and was soon afterward expelled from the Writers' Union. Daniel, perhaps out of deference to his distinguished war record, was given five years. Neither man was given any term of exile.

The verdict provoked a storm of indignation outside the Soviet Union and considerable reaction within. Telegrams and letters arrived from writers, scientists and intellectuals in all parts of the world. There were appeals from the PEN club centers of Iceland, India, Iran, protests from Japan, Mexico, Argentina, Paraguay, Australia and the Philippines, as well as from the countries of Western Europe. There were even reactions from Eastern Europe, a letter of protest from Polish university teachers, to cite one of a necessarily limited number of examples. The statement of the French poet Louis Aragon, published in the organ of the

French communist party, *L'Humanité*, is a typical expression of the shock experienced the communist parties of western Europe: "But to deprive them of liberty because of the contents of their novels or short stories is to make a crime out of misdemeanour of opinion and to set a precedent more harmful to socialism than their works could ever be." [10]

Within the Soviet Union adverse reaction to the verdict was not limited to the ranks of writers and the artists. Letters were sent by mathematicians, economists, linguists, and members of other professions, a fact which points in several directions. It proves that Sinyavsky had been read or, after his trial, was being read by a widening circle of the Soviet intelligentsia; that Soviet intellectuals were not intimidated by the trial but, on the contrary, were moved to protest it; that scientists understood that the repression of two writers was not an isolated event, but one that had implications for the Soviet scientific community, which was waging its own campaign for greater freedom and which had itself experienced a sort of Socialist Realism in science under the reign of Lysenko.

Of course, there was support for the sentence within the Soviet Union. The Union of Soviet Writers issued a statement on February 19, 1966, in *Literaturnaya gazeta:*

Together with the Soviet people as a whole, Soviet writers support their state, as they always have and as they always will. . . . This, precisely, is why we disapprove and are indignant at the vile deeds of Sinyavsky and Daniel, and why we approve the sentence passed by the court in accordance with the spirit and the letter of our laws.[11]

This statement could by no means have enjoyed the unanimous support of the entire membership for sixty-three Moscow writers, all members of the Writers' Union, and including such figures as Chukovsky, Ehrenburg, Shklovsky, Nagibin, and Okudzhava sent their own letter of protest to the Presidium of the 23rd Congress of the CPSU, the Supreme Soviet of the USSR, and the Supreme Soviet of the RSFSR, concluding:

We beg you therefore to release Andrey Sinyavsky and Yuli Daniel on our surety.

This would be an act dictated by the interests of the country, the interests of peace and those of the world communist movement.[12]

No Soviet writer of any consequence supported the court's decision with the exception of Mikhail Sholokhov, who had attacked Pasternak when he won the Nobel Prize and who was later to attack Solzhenitsyn when he won his. In *On Socialist Realism*, Sinyavsky speaks with fondness of the romantic side of the Revolution ("the rattling of sabers and the neighing of horses, the shootings without judgment and without consequences"), a fondness which Sholokhov seems to share:

If these fellows with the black consciences had been caught in the memorable twenties, when people were not tried on the basis of closely defined articles of the criminal code, then, good heavens, they would have got something quite different, these turncoats! But now, if you please, people talk about the sentence being too harsh.[13]

In Sholokhov's final phrase we see the reserve clause of the hard-liners: if verdicts like this one fail to stem the tide of treasonous literature, it is only because they are insufficiently severe.

Sinyavsky and Daniel were not made to drink hemlock like Socrates, nor burned at the stake like Giordano Bruno,[14] but their trial resembled those of the other two in that they were tried not for crimes but for ideas or, more precisely, for ideas the rulers found criminal. Sinyavsky did not confront the system with a new world-view, as did Bruno when he espoused the cosmology of Copernicus, for, as Sinyavsky knew all too well, his was not the age to generate a new world-view; Sinyavsky did confront the system with an allegiance to its visionary ideals, when what was required was fidelity to the party line; with a vision that included the social world and found room for personal and metaphysical concerns as well, when what was required was homage to the vision of man as a completely historical phenomenon. The true forces of resistance in the Soviet Union today are neither anti-Soviet nor apolitical. Having moved through politics and history to points beyond, they may best be termed parapolitical; in that respect, they are utterly different from forces at work in the West, for the Soviet dissidence is based on a too intimate knowledge of history, whereas too often Western rebellion is based on willful ignorance masquerading as innocence. Aleksander Wat, the Polish futurist poet, who was critical of Sinyavsky's early works, in the end comes to the following conclusion:

In order to liberate themselves from Stalin's heritage *in their souls*, they must first "detach themselves from the enemy"; like a snake sheds its skin in the springtime, they must throw off not only any concern with Stalinism, Communism, revisionism, but those ugly words themselves. In this sense, the free people are not Andrey Voznesensky, Evtushenko, or Tarsis but such people as the poet Joseph Brodsky, as Solzhenitsyn of *Matryona's House*, as Tertz-Sinyavsky of his last (apolitical!) works. For political thinking has become so distorted and so depraved during the long, long half-century, that one has to begin with tearing it out, together with its roots, from one's soul, so that the ground be prepared for a political thing, healthy, humane, which makes for the *virtu* of a free citizen. Anticommunists in the West do not understand this. Of course, acts of political rebellion and, even more, a political rebellion of the mind, are useful, for they squeeze concessions from the rulers, but nevertheless in the Russian Empire they will remain—for many years to come—abortive, powerless to touch off a movement of the masses; personally I see the hope of Russia not in them but in life itself, in existence (*Sein*) in an utterly different spiritual space.[15]

3

On Socialist Realism

The death of the great tyrant and the reading of the list of his crimes shook the entire communist world. The new era was quickly tagged "the Thaw" (from Ilya Ehrenburg's novel of that title), an image suggesting hope and rebirth and, by implication, defining Stalinism in winter's metaphors of ice and darkness. Both of these seasons of history were to become themes in Sinyavsky's work. For a time the situation remained relatively fluid and shook with waves of liberated energy. The Poles brought back Gomulka and carefully but boldly started out on a Polish road to socialism. The Hungarians went too far, and the crushing of their uprising was a signal that Soviet tanks still defined the limits of the new era. In the USSR itself there were stirrings, soul-searchings, and a sense that martyrdom, though still inevitable, could now be had at a lesser price, all of which were later to coalesce into what is now known as the dissident movement. But it is essential to understand the hierarchy of power in the communist world in order to appreciate the position of Andrei Sinyavsky in 1956. For a great many reasons, nationalism not the least of them, the relationship of the countries of Eastern Europe to Moscow can be viewed as a game of give and take, the idea being, of course, to take more from Moscow than must be given, a relationship which parallels that between the intelligentsia and the regime in any communist country. But in the center of power the relationship is not marked by such clarity; it is easily clouded by loyalty to the ideals of the Revolution, Russian patriotism, a simple lack of information for making intelligent comparisons, or the certainty that what is barely permissible in Warsaw is strictly forbidden in Moscow. With that in mind we can compare Sinyavsky's *On Socialist Realism* with similar works written at the same time. Though they are more or less equal as far as audacity is concerned, Sinyavsky's work is in some respects less blunt and direct than Adam Ważyk's "Poem for Adults" or Leszek Kołakowski's "What is Socialism," which shares its tone of ironic outrage. The latter work had been scheduled for publication in *Po Prostu* before that journal was banned in 1957. Sinyavsky, however, was aware from the start that his work would not even enjoy the luxury of being prohibited, and immediately chose the underground course that, ironically, the writers of the freer socialist countries would be forced to take in time. Sinyavsky's choice of secrecy and a pseudonym sets him apart from his colleagues in the Soviet Union who were trying to thread their way between the demands of politics and the claims of art. His allegiance to unadulterated creative freedom served Sinyavsky well, for it was he, and not those like Yevtushenko, who made too many compromises, who found the way to the heart of his time; for that reason, to compare Sinyavsky's work with that of his contemporaries, with the exception, of course, of Solzhenitsyn and a few others, is not particularly profitable, for they were operating on different levels. The same may be said of comparing the writings of Sinyavsky and Tertz; the world of the former is cramped by caution, whereas in the latter there are no boundaries to the imaginative space nor to the play of the imagination itself.

For Sinyavsky, *On Socialist Realism*, his first work, was both an end and a beginning. An end because it was obviously the product of a long, painful, complex confrontation with Soviet reality, Russian literature, and himself. It marked a stage in his development which could permit no turning back. It was a beginning because it led logically and inevitably to his subsequent works which succeed in embodying the new aesthetic position announced at the close of the essay.

Though it is a remarkable document and in many ways artistically superior to his first novel, *The Trial Begins*, its present significance for Russian literature is almost impossible to assess. We know that it has circulated in the underground in *samizdat* editions. Sinyavsky's influence on Daniel is clear enough, yet we do not know how Sinyavsky's conclusions affected other members of the disaffiliated intelligentsia. Certainly there must be those who simply disagree with his conclusion that only a phantasmagoric and grotesque art can adequately mimic the bizarre convolutions of the past and the present. The work of Solzhenitsyn, for example, is close in form to the type of literature Sinyavsky rejects; but many good reasons can be advanced for each man's choice of form, and the novels of Solzhenitsyn may well be an exception, an old form redeemed by talent and moral passion. In any case, debate on this subject would necessarily have hinged on whether Sinyavsky's grotesque hyperboles produce yet another distortion of the human image, or whether they represent a new mutation of the spirit, the exaltation of subjectivity countering a planned economy, an orthodox ideology, and the worship of "objectivity."

Though there is little evidence as to the impact of Sinyavsky's underground writings on other Russian writers or on the intelligentsia in general, we do possess one detailed account of their influence, a short critical study of Abram Tertz by the Yugoslav writer Mihajlo Mihajlov, *Escape from the Test Tube* (*Begstvo iz retorty* in its Russian émigré translation). The book was written in 1965 shortly before Sinyavsky was arrested, while Mihajlov himself was in a Yugoslav jail. Though Mihajlov had not read *On Socialist Realism* but only *The Trial Begins* and *Fantastic Stories*, the fruits of Sinyavsky's new aesthetic made an enormous impression on him. The time and the place are important here, the mid-sixties and Yugoslavia, the freest of the socialist countries. Sinyavsky's writing came as a revelation to Mihajlov:

A miracle has happened! In the intervals between the two interrogations and my daily walk along the fenced-in roof of the prison, a great, original, and unique talent was revealed to me, I encountered a vision of the world unusually familiar and yet completely new, whose significance for contemporary literature, and, in particular, for Russian literature is immeasurably great. . . . Its significance can only be compared with that of Franz Kafka for European literature at the middle of this century.[1]

If this is the impression made by Sinyavsky's works on a sophisticated and widely read critic like Mihajlov, who quotes freely from Buber and Rozanov, one can assume that Russians would react with at least equal intensity. But analogies are not evidence.

In any case, *On Socialist Realism* [2] notified readers outside the Soviet Union that a brilliant new figure had arisen in Russian literature and was preserving his safety under the pseudonym Abram Tertz. This essay was given wide and immediate European publication in 1959, appearing in *L'Esprit, Kultura,* and *Il Tempo Presente.* After first appearing in *Dissent,* it was published in book form in English in 1960 with a preface by Czesław Miłosz. Guesses as to the author's identity began at once. Some critics attempted to identify him with known Soviet authors, whereas others were content to draw a generalized portrait of Tertz on the basis of his first two published works.[3] Miłosz, for example, concluded: "All the evidence goes to show, however, that he belongs to the younger generation of Russian writers, educated entirely under the postrevolutionary system." [4] Similar conclusions were drawn in the April 1962 edition of *Survey* by Aleksander Wat, writing under the pen name of Stefan Bergholz. Wat went further than identifying Tertz's age, class, and background: he found fault with his intellectual vocabulary and the very processes of his thinking, considering them as yet unliberated from the confines of a Soviet education, criticisms which will be taken up later on. But arrest and trial made any more guessing superfluous.

On Socialist Realism, besides affording aesthetic pleasures, presents some intellectual hazards, since it is as much a polemical work as an analytical one. Furthermore, since Sinyavsky's principal tool of exposition is irony, the reader must be very careful in abstracting specific conclusions. Irony and sincerity are sometimes difficult to differentiate in his writings; sincerity comes masked in irony and irony uses sincerity as its sheep's clothing. The real problem, of course, is that Sinyavsky does not yet have definite attitudes and this first work of his is an attempt to order conflicting emotions, conflicting ideas. The "nervous" zigzagging of the line of thought, the use of vivid metaphoric language, and the refusal to present ideas solely in logical and dispassionate form makes the work all the more enjoyable and, in fact, it belongs to that small body of critical literature which can be read as much for pleasure as for instruction.

The author himself divides the essay into three parts, each of which views the central problem, the relation between literature and reality, in a different context. The first section is distinctly philosophical, the second is concerned with history and the history of Russian literature, and the concluding section moves toward a programmatic stance. To a considerable degree, the development of this essay mirrors Sinyavsky's development as a writer—the move-ment is from the abstract to the particular, from the philo-sophic to the historical, and the polemics on art becomes a polemical art.

The first section is centered on the teleological nature and needs of the human mind. Sinyavsky argues that the need for a sense of purpose is intrinsic and that religion is the traditional means of satisfying that need. His argument reduced to its bare bones runs as follows: Christianity has been discredited by its historical success as an institution and by its failure to redeem mankind, just as the vision of the free, creative individual, born in the Renaissance, failed to inspire Western Europeans to transcend the meaner limitations of human nature. But man needs to feel that daily life moves in conjuction with a higher order, that actions are not random but part of a greater pattern, not purposeless but part of a larger purpose. Communism is the only ideal that has arisen in the spiritual vacuum of the modern age. Sinyavsky lays great stress on communism as an ideal for he is to build his discussion on the discrepancies between the ideal and the practice, or, in his terms, the ends and the means. Soviet society as the vessel of communism, and Soviet culture as its expression, must be thoroughly teleological: "Our art, like our culture, is teleological through and through. It is subject to a higher destiny, by which it is ennobled. In the last analysis we live only to speed the coming of communism." [5]

The teleological side of Soviet life did not escape Solzhenitsyn either. In *The First Circle*, in the chapter entitled *Language as a Means of Production*, Stalin is described in the act of contemplation:

"The superstructure was created by the base *for the purpose of* . . ."
"Language was created *for the purpose of* . . ."
His brownish-gray, smallpox-pitted face, with its great plow of a nose, bent low over the sheet of paper, and he did not see the angel of medieval teleology smiling over his shoulder.[6]

A teleological system that does not include a margin of doubt by which to recognize the supreme complexity of existence can be, in practice, tragic, in theory, comic. By logically extending Marxist historicism and its claims to universality to prehistoric times, Sinyavsky reduces it to absurdity: "The ape stoop up on its hind legs and began its triumphant procession toward communism." [7] As we shall soon see, Sinyavsky's real concern is with the dialectical interplay of means and ends, but in passing it is worth pointing out that he is touching here one of communism's sore spots, namely, its cosmic provincialism. Seen against either the expanding universe of astrophysics or its microscopic twin of the cell and the atom, Marxism's human—all-too-human—limitations are discomfortingly apparent (a fact which explains why Teilhard de Chardin, who has attempted to unite God, evolution, and history into a single vision, is popular in the countries of Eastern Europe).

Sinyavsky's opening move, as we have seen, is to describe Soviet communism as a religion born out of the great spiritual hunger of the Russian nineteenth century. In his view, by no means unique, communism qualifies as a religion because of its teleological nature, its claim to universality, and its ideals, which are largely a secularized version of Christianity. As a religion it must, by its nature, take the position that its truth excludes all others, that is, it must sharply distinguish between the faithful and the enemies of the faith, between orthodoxy and heresy: "True faith is not compatible with tolerance. Neither is it compatible with historicism, i.e., with tolerance applied to the past." [8] Thus, fanaticism is inevitable. As mentioned before, this fanaticism has two roots, one reaching back into Russian history, the other issuing from the very nature of religious systems. Two quotations will illustrate his views on this subject:

The great hunger of the nineteenth century perhaps conditioned us Russians to throw ourselves so greedily upon the food prepared by Marx and to devour it even before we had time to analyze its taste, smell, and consequences. But this hundred years' hunger was itself caused by the catastrophic absence of food: it was a hunger of godlessness.[9]

Even the most liberal God offers only one freedom of choice: to believe or not to believe, to be for Him or for Satan, to go to paradise or to hell. Communism offers just about the same right. If you don't want to believe you can go to jail—which is by no means worse than hell.[10]

Confronted by the tragedy of communism, Sinyavsky is desperately seeking its cause, and he finds three distinct, but related causes. The line of reasoning examined above culminates in a bitter and ironic passage which yields insights into both communism and the workings of Sinyavsky's mind:

So that prisons should vanish forever, we built new prisons. So that all frontiers should fall, we surrounded ourselves with a Chinese Wall. So that work should become relaxing and a pleasure, we introduced forced labor. So that not one drop of blood be shed any more, we killed and killed and killed.

In the name of the Purpose we turned to the means that our enemies used: we glorified Imperial Russia, we wrote lies in *Pravda* [Truth], we set a new Tsar on the now empty throne, we introduced officers' epaulettes and tortures. . . . Sometimes we felt that only one final sacrifice was needed for the triumph of Communism—the renunciation of Communism.

O Lord, O Lord, forgive us our sins! [11]

Though this passage crackles with dialectic wit, its essential message, that of the diabolical confusion of ends and means, is quite simple and accords with the position taken by members of the loyal opposition like Isaac Deutscher, who wrote in his *The Unfinished Revolution:* "In the course of the advance, which was made for Russia far more difficult than it need have been by wars, arms races, and bureaucratic waste, ever new contradictions arose; and means and ends were perpetually confused." [12] The important thing here is that both Deutscher's and Sinyavsky's arguments cite contingencies whose absence would have resulted in a different picture; for Deutscher those contingencies are war, arms races, and so forth, and for Sinyavsky, the spiritual hunger of the nineteenth century, which ensured the fanaticism of communism triumphant. Though Sinyavsky discusses Dostoevsky's assertion that human nature is too broad to devote itself exclusively to one faith, thus developing a second criticism of communism, namely, that as a world-view it is necessarily in opposition to the intractable variety of life, he never deals with Dostoevsky's metaphysical critique of socialism. That critique may be briefly summarized as follows: the inquisitions of Catholicism contradict its basic spirit, the spirit of Christ, the spirit of love and of respect for the individual human soul. Socialism, on the other hand, denies the individual soul, locates its own first principle in the impersonal forces of history, and thus under socialism the individual becomes simply part of a vast machine and has no value except in relation to that machine. For that reason, the inquisitions of socialism are not a betrayal of its basic spirit and premises but their inevitable consequence. Ends and means, far from being confused, are, in fact, in perfect harmony. At this stage, Sinyavsky is still too caught up in a tangle of loyalties and old habits of mind to be able to confront socialism with that ultimate challenge.

The mental acrobatics of the last-quoted passages from *On Socialist Realism* have a value of their own. The line of thought in those passages, in which dialectics are battled with dialectics, betrays Sinyavsky's Marxist education, for Sinyavsky has yet to learn that communism can be countered only from some point outside itself, not from within. For that reason, Wat's criticism of him is valid: "Tertz is not only the analyst of his country's particular situation,

but also its product. He has unconsciously taken over from
the ideologists of Marxism that imprecision and ambiguity
in basic concepts which they deliberately exploit." [13] In
time, Sinyavsky was to purge himself of that confusion, liberating himself from his own conditioning within the limits
to which that is possible. There is a hint of Sinyavsky's escape route from the maze and *lager* of Marxist thought in
the paragraph that ends: "Sometimes we felt that only one
final sacrifice was needed for the triumph of Communism—
the renunciation of Communism. O Lord, O Lord, forgive
us our sins!" In the same way that he ridiculed Marxism's
teleology, he ridicules dialectical thinking by means of
reductio ad absurdum, a process that contains the seeds of
liberation, and for further comic effects he encloses one
teleology (Marxism) within another (Christianity). Such
toying with *Weltanschauungen* is characteristic of men educated in the ideologically saturated atmosphere of Eastern
Europe, and it is no coincidence that Wat (at first Sinyavsky's critic, later his admirer, himself a man who struggled
free of communism), in his poem "Japanese Archery" [14]
achieves the same comic effect by the sudden inclusion of
one total world-view within another:

I.

The hand tells the bowstring:
    Obey me.
The bowstring answers the hand:
    Draw valiantly.
The bowstring tells the arrow:
    O arrow, fly.
The arrow answers the bowstring:

Speed my flight.
The arrow tells the target:
    Be my light.
The target answers the arrow:
    Love me.

2.

The target tells arrow, bowstring, hand and eye:
    Ta twam asi.
Which means in a sacred language:
    I am Thou.

3.

(Footnote of a Christian:
    O Mother of God,
Watch over the target, the bow, the arrow
    And the archer).

In discussing the history of literature Sinyavsky does not make X-rays of aesthetic structures, but instead reads the spiritual and historical life of his country by examining the symbols, characters, and situations created by its literature. In the criticism he published in the Soviet Union, Sinyavsky has always accorded taste a position of prominence, though even as a critic his concern has extended beyond aesthetics because taste to him implies a sense of reality more complex than that allowed by the official guidelines. In *On Socialist Realism*, mediocre works are often given as much attention as masterpieces, for the former are equally as indicative of the character of the times as the latter and, during a certain stretch of Soviet history, perhaps even more indicative. This approach, a sort of anthropological criticism in which literary works are treated as artifacts, is part of the tradition of Russian literary criticism; its strength is that, by treating works of literature as more than clever toys, it enforces a certain seriousness and sense of artistic responsibility; its weakness is that, since it obscures the distinction between social relevance and artistic merit, it promotes a climate in which, as we have already seen from Sinyavsky's trial, the fictive and individual aspects of literature can be wholly lost sight of.

By locating the roots of teleological fanaticism and its literary extension, Socialist Realism, in the spiritual wasteland of the nineteenth century, Sinyavsky half accepts one of the canons of Soviet literary criticism: the writer in pre-revolutionary Russia was necessarily alienated from the society in which he lived because that society was brutal and unjust (this canon, of course, needs a few dependent clauses to explain reactionary writers like Dostoevsky). In any case, it is a decent enough generalization, but, as Sinyavsky demonstrates, it doesn't hold for the eighteenth century; its corollary, that the Soviet writer need not be alienated from his society, that he can in fact be its spiritual leader, an "engineer of souls," does not appear at all groundless to Sinyavsky who treats this problem seriously and at some length; to follow the path of his reasoning is to enter that private desert where Soviet intellectuals wrestle with their demons.

In the nineteenth century, which Sinyavsky characterizes as "atheistic, tolerant, disoriented" and "soft and shriveled, feminine and melancholy, full of doubts, inner contradictions, and pangs of conscience," [15] the character type which contains the essence of the time is the so-called superfluous man, who is unable to live a purposeful life and who dissipates his energies in noble fantasies and rhetoric. His impotence, due both to the implacable society around him and a lack of faith within, is portrayed not in political contexts (which were tabu) but in amorous ones. As Sinyavsky points out, love and politics were often synonymous in the Aesopian language of nineteenth-century Russian literature; it is a device Sinyavsky himself uses in *The Trial Begins*, where the means versus ends argument is miniaturized into a love affair that ends in impotence, not union. This generalization too has its weaknesses—Tolstoy's Pierre Bezukhov in *War and Peace* was a superfluous man who found fulfillment in a love that was not a political allegory but a symbol of the abiding forces of daily life.

The principal psychological characteristic of the superfluous man is his addiction to irony. This particular form of irony is, as Alexander Blok defined it, a spiritual malady, and derives both from a painful perception of discrepancy (between a man's ideals and his actions, between his hopes and reality) and a lack of any faith strong enough to unite irony's double perspective. Sinyavsky sets irony and faith against each other:

Irony is the language of the superfluous man who derides both himself and everything sacred in the world. . . . Irony is the faithful companion of unbelief and doubt; it vanishes as soon as there appears a faith that does not tolerate sacrilege.[16]

To what degree, one wonders, does this definition reflect its maker? After all, Sinyavsky even tips his hand when he says: "While working on this article I have caught myself more than once dropping into irony—that unworthy device!" [17] But his irony should not be confused with that of the superfluous man, even though Sinyavsky may seem to be suffering from similar symptoms and moving toward a similar position outside society. The superfluous man uses irony to defend himself against a monstrous world and his own inner weakness, but the irony is corrosive and in time infects the hand that wields it. For Sinyavsky, irony is not so much a means of defense as a tool of aggression, to be used in hacking his way out of society, freeing his mind and soul from the thought patterns and values which had formed him since early youth. At this stage, he does not envision a new set of values and is more concerned with understanding and rebelling against those which still have a hold on him. Sinyavsky's thinking is occasionally blurred as a result of his Marxist education, as Wat has charged, but this blurring is also the product of his self-liberation, which Wat fails to notice. Sinyavsky has never abandoned irony but, in harmony with his own development, has refined it from hostile sarcasm into a unique blend of impertinence and serenity.

The superfluous man as both a social and a literary type (the terms are essentially interchangeable in Sinyavsky's use of them) is more out of place in the twentieth century than he was in the nineteenth:

The superfluous man seemed . . . much more dangerous than the openly negative enemy. After all, the enemy was like the positive hero—clear, straightforward, and, in his own way, purposeful. Only his significance was negative—to hinder the movement to the Purpose. But the superfluous man was a creature of different psychological dimensions, inaccessible to computation and regimentation. He is neither for the Purpose nor against the Purpose—he is outside the Purpose. . . . He proclaims that there are no Reds and no Whites but simply people, poor, unfortunate, superfluous people.[18]

This is, in embryo, the position Sinyavsky himself is now striving for, though he still has only the faintest idea of what his destination will be. The superfluous man, in the nineteenth century the result of an implacable society which refused its progressive and idealistic members any role whatsoever, now by an irony of history becomes an ideal, a refuge of humanity and sanity outside the deadly either/or mentality of Soviet society, though now there is a heightened emphasis on inner freedom, inner strength. Andrei Amalrik is driving at much the same thing when, in his open letter to Anatoli Kuznetsov discussing the works of contemporary Soviet writers, he remarks: "I suggest that they are not Soviet and not anti-Soviet, but simply literature which wishes to be free." [19]

Sinyavsky notes three phases in Soviet literature—the ebullient, innovative twenties, the ice age of Socialist Realism, and a new phase arising out of the turmoil of the Thaw. His attitude toward the Romantic literature of the twenties is mixed; he views it with great respect because it is so brilliant and so much a part of the Revolution whose memory "is as sacred . . . as the image of a dead mother," but he also treats it ironically, keeping it at a distance so not to succumb to its charm and verve, which did correspond to the spirit of the twenties but hardly does to that of the fifties. Both in his criticism and his fiction Sinyavsky often returns to the twenties in order to find a context for certain problematic writers like Pasternak and Akhmatova, and to mend the severed tradition of Russian literature, but he tries to avoid what he considers the traps of Romanticism. His adverse criticism of Soviet literature in that decade can also be read as a tongue-in-cheek defense of it since he assumes a quasi-official view when damning the excesses of Romanticism. What Sinyavsky takes from the Romanticism of the twenties is its innovative daring, its tendency toward exaggeration, its energy as opposed to the entropy of Socialist Realism, to use Zamiatin's terms; what he rejects is the romantic tendency to take "the wish for the reality." Much as Sinyavsky longs to wake from the nightmare of history, he has too much respect for history to deny its power and presence; for that reason, his stories, no matter how formally or philosophically bold, are always rooted in a definite social milieu. In fact, his satire is built of the play of mundane and vulgar reality against the fantastic strangeness of the human soul and so, unlike the Romantics, Sinyavsky makes a humorous device of alienation; his primary comic perception derives from a certain wonder, a question—how could such an extraordinary creature as man have ended up creating such a drab and miserable world?

Sinyavsky sees the passage from the free literature of the twenties to government-imposed Socialist Realism as mirroring a fundamental change in Soviet society. To some degree he considers formalization inevitable, given the history and shape of revolutionary mentality combined with the success of the Revolution. Some of his metaphors—Romanticism as youth, revolutionaries grown fat—suggest a natural process familiar to the sociologists of institutions: a group tends to be relatively flexible and dynamic when it is outside the main currents of a society and during the early phase of its ascendancy, but, once its position is established, it tends to grow increasingly conservative, and its original goals are supplanted by the desire for self-perpetuation. It is essential to note that Sinyavsky does not quarrel with the basic assumption of Socialist Realism, that under socialism the alienation of the writer could end because his interests and those of society become identical. At this point Sinyavsky parts company with those Western intellectuals for whom a reconciliation of literature and society is anathema. Elsewhere, and here by implication, Sinyavsky rebukes them for their constant scepticism, which has no roots in the religious dimension of the mind and is therefore incapable of inspiring man with visions of unity.

Sinyavsky attributes the failure of Socialist Realism to three distinct causes, one historical, one philosophical, one literary. First, there was the "failure" of success, which changed artistic expression from a Romantic to a classical mode, purging it of the doubts, complexities, and bitter afterthoughts found in Russian literature since the nineteenth century. It succeeded in making the new work resemble the Russian literature of the eighteenth century, which was abstract, rhetorical, self-confident, close to the state, all of which he sums up in the metaphoric formula: "The river of art was covered with the ice of classicism."

Second, he does not view the unity of society and art as something unnatural or unprecedented:

Art is not afraid of dictatorships, severity, repressions, or even conservatism and clichés. When necessary, art can be narrowly religious, dumbly governmental, devoid of individuality—and yet good. We go into aesthetic raptures over the stereotypes of Egyptian art, Russian icons and folklore.[20]

But such a political-religious system must spellbind its citizens with numinous goals, images, and charismatic leaders. In other words, it must never for an instant be revealed as a human institution, for it would thus instantly lose its power, basis, and raison d'être:

The strength of a teleological system resides in its constancy, harmony, and order. Once we admit that God carelessly sinned with Eve and, becoming jealous of Adam, sent him off to labor at land reclamation, the whole concept of the Creation falls apart, and it is impossible to restore the faith.[21]

In a passage of splendid irony, whose comic implications touch upon the fallibility and pretentiousness of communism as religion and upon the Russian weakness for deifying their leaders, Sinyavsky indicates the fatal error that doomed the communist mystique and with it Socialist Realism:

The death of Stalin inflicted an irreparable loss upon our religious-aesthetic system; it cannot be resuscitated through the now revived cult of Lenin. Lenin is too much like an ordinary man and his image is too realistic: small, bald, dressed in civilian clothes. Stalin seemed to be specially made for the hyperbole that awaited him: mysterious, omniscient, all-powerful, he was the living monument of our era and needed only one quality to become God—immortality.

Ah, if only we had been intelligent enough to surround his death with miracles! We could have announced on the radio that he did not die but had risen to Heaven, from which he continued to watch us, in silence, no words emerging from beneath his mystic moustache. His relics would have cured men struck by paralysis or possessed by demons. And children, before going to bed, would have kneeled by the window and addressed their prayers to the cold shining stars of the Celestial Kremlin.[22]

And yet the passage contains some genuine regret, a sense of loss, for the death of Stalin did, in fact, mean a "lessening" of Soviet society, a return to dull, collective sobriety. Irrational, yet very human, the impulse here is like that which makes a man who has never seen war long for it. As Sinyavsky remarked in conversation with Aucouturier: "When Stalin was alive it cost one something to think, it was dangerous, one was frightened, now, it's going to become too easy." [23]

Finally, approaching Socialist Realism from a strictly literary point of view, Sinyavsky asserts that the work of Mayakovsky, "the most socialist realist of all," proves by its very existence that excellent literature can be written in harmony with society and the state. Nevertheless, Sinyavsky fails to ask two questions that would be most pertinent: Wasn't Mayakovsky's art essentially a spontaneous response to the age issuing from his own temperament, talent, and vision, and, if so, why should one assume that other writers would be able to take his vision for their own? Didn't Mayakovsky's suicide in 1930 signal his despair at the direction Soviet society and Soviet literature were taking? In any case, Sinyavsky decides that the blame for the failure of Socialist Realism must fall on "the writers who accepted the rules of Socialist Realism but did not have sufficient artistic consistency to embody them in deathless images. Mayakovsky had that consistency." [24]

But Sinyavsky himself is somewhat inconsistent since, on the one hand, he blames the writers for the failure of Socialist Realism and, on the other, he blames contradictions in the very theoretical structure of the concept itself. The "loathsome literary salad" which Socialist Realism became was the result of eclecticism, the attempt to breed creatures of utterly different species, the realism of the nineteenth century with its fidelity to psychological nuance and visual details based on observations of specific milieus, and the stylized, hyperbolic religious art which was a response to the teleological imperatives of socialism:

Mayakovsky knew this and, hating psychological analysis and details, wrote in proportions that were larger than life. He wrote coarsely, poster-style, Homerically. . . . If socialist realism really wants to rise to the level of the great world cultures and produce its *Communiad*, there is only one way to do it. It must give up the "realism," renounce the sorry and fruitless attempts to write a socialist *Anna Karenina* or a socialist *Cherry Orchard*. When it abandons its efforts to achieve verisimilitude, it will be able to express the grand and implausible sense of our era.[25]

Apart from any questions as to the causes of the decline and fall of communist teleology and Socialist Realism, in the end, Sinyavsky and his society find themselves in a situation very much resembling the spiritual impasse of the West, though they have traveled a very different road to arrive there. In the nineteenth century, living under an outmoded system, Russian writers were somehow in touch with the most vital currents of the age and the age to come. A similar paradox holds for the present; out of nowhere two Russian writers, Sinyavsky and Solzhenitsyn, have appeared, one to take his place in the vanguard of world literature, the other to shame modern writing with his depth, range, and moral authority.

Having concluded that "today's children will scarcely be able to produce a new God capable of inspiring humanity into the next historical cycle," Sinyavsky finds that this historical interlude has qualities of its own that require new modes of perception, a new art. To some degree the art he invokes at the end of *On Socialist Realism* in a passage he appended after having shipped the manuscript out of the Soviet Union, resembles the Socialist Realism that failed to materialize, just as Solzhenitsyn's novels contain much that would have suited the canons of Socialist Realism. But the differences are, of course, great and decisive, and not the least among them is Sinyavsky's absence of Purpose.

Right now I put my hope in a phantasmagoric art, with hypotheses instead of a Purpose, an art in which the grotesque will replace realistic descriptions of ordinary life. Such an art would correspond best to the spirit of our time. May the fantastic imagery of Hoffmann and Dostoevsky, of Goya, Chagall, and Mayakovsky (the most socialist realist of all), and of many other realists and nonrealists teach us how to be truthful with the aid of the absurd and the fantastic.

Having lost our faith, we have not lost our enthusiasm about the metamorphoses of God that take place before our very eyes, the miraculous transformations of His entrails and His cerebral convolutions. We don't know where to go; but, realizing that there is nothing to be done about it, we start to think, to set riddles, to make assumptions. May we thus invent something marvelous? Perhaps, but it will no longer be socialist realism.[26]

One may agree or disagree with Sinyavsky's version of Russian history and the course of Russian literature, but his vision has an importance that transcends its correctness or fallibility; *On Socialist Realism* is as much a testament, a record of an unfinished struggle, as a work of critical analysis, and for readers outside the Soviet Union it provides a rare glimpse of the thought patterns of a Soviet intellectual. Andrei Amalrik said that his book *Will the Soviet Union Survive until 1984?* has for students of Russia "the same interest as a fish would for ichthyologists if it all of a sudden began to talk"; [27] in this and all of Sinyavsky's subsequent work, we not only hear the fish speak, but witness its evolution as well.

4

The Trial Begins

The Trial Begins was written in the same year as *On Socialist Realism*. Even the most cursory examination of the two works will reveal their common concern and internal similarities. It is possible that Sinyavsky worked on both of them at the same time, but it seems to me more likely that he worked out the main principles of his argument in the essay before trying his hand at fictionalizing his ideas. In any case, it is best to speak of the novel as a continuation of the essay in a different genre, the artistic concerns of the essay having given the novel its shape, and the philosophical concerns having become the characters and the plot. And, of course, this novel must be viewed against the artistic credo which Sinyavsky announced at the end of his essay *On Socialist Realism*, for all his subsequent writings were an attempt to realize that vision in the flesh of fiction.

Bizarre and experimental as *The Trial Begins* may be, especially in Soviet terms, it is nothing but a modern mutation of the historical novel (though Walter Scott, the founder of that school, might have some trouble recognizing the genre he fathered). It deals with a definite historical period and a genuine incident, with actual characters appearing in the background of the narrative, and the lovers' trials are not only private matters, but personify historical dilemmas as well. Thus, the characteristics of the historical novel, as identified by Lukács [1] and others, are present in *The Trial Begins*. But Sinyavsky, who has begun his experiments with form, has so modified the means of narration that the shape of the genre is not immediately recognizable.

In 1952 Stalin's regime was under considerable stress. Relations with the United States were particularly bad. Tito, in a speech in Bosnia, bitterly attacked the Soviet Union; he defended himself and Yugoslavia against Stalin's accusations, which he called only an effort to mask the vicious crimes and broken promises of the regime. The Soviet Union was experiencing internal difficulties as well. The masses were grumbling about shortages of food, clothing, and housing. Molotov, Kaganovich, Mikoyan, and Beria urged Stalin to begin another wave of purges, but he was hesitant, preferring the idea of a Party Congress. A Party Congress, the first in thirteen years, might serve to divert attention from the country's domestic and foreign difficulties, Stalin thought. In the end, however, he fell back on the use of the purge, and one was begun in the winter of 1952–1953. [2]

It was decided in the Kremlin that the purge needed a focus, a center for public attention, and so the Doctors' Plot was hatched. On January 13, 1953, Tass and Radio Moscow announced the uncovering of the murder of two Soviet leaders and a plot to kill others, including Stalin, by medical means. The ringleaders were identified as a group of nine doctors and specialists, six of whom were Jewish. They supposedly had confessed to being paid agents of the British and Americans and to having killed Andrei Zhdanov in 1948 and, in 1945, Shcherbakov, director of the political administration of the Red Army. The doctors were also said to be connected to "Joint," a philanthropic organization originally set up to help Jewish war victims. A press campaign against Zionists and the state of Israel was linked up with the campaign against "rootless cosmopolitans" that had begun earlier, all of which provided the official fanfare for terror. The death of Stalin on March 5, 1953, put an end to that campaign. Still, its effects were felt for a long time afterward, as was indicated by Andrei Amalrik in his book *Involuntary Journey to Siberia*, which depicts peasants afraid of doctors with "non-Russian" names, who are rumored to drain patients of their blood and sell it.[3]

The Trial Begins is Sinyavsky's attempt to catch the psychology and atmosphere of "the dark and magical night of Stalin's dictatorship." The key word here is "magical," which indicates Sinyavsky's basic intuition about Stalinism: since the dictator was paranoid and had created a paranoid structure around him to carry out his will, producing a sort of national psychosis, it would be almost impossible for a writer to reproduce either the psychology of the time or its machinations by using the literary method called realism. Realism is primarily a method of representing the familiar visual and social world. The magical world, which is neither visible nor familiar, is closer to the logic of dreams and obsessions than to everyday reality. However, Sinyavsky's method should not be confused with surrealism, which is essentially a response to Freud's discovery of the Atlantis of the unconscious, an effort to explore that realm with utter disregard for the world experienced in the waking state. Sinyavsky, like most Russian writers of this century and the last, can hardly afford the luxury of purely subjective musings: history has become for him too much a part of the riddle of the world. It is precisely the interplay of personality and society, consciousness and atmosphere that interests Sinyavsky at this stage.

Sinyavsky has no doubt read the Formalists and familiarized himself with their theory of *ostranenie* (making things strange), which holds that human perceptions, through repetition, become dulled and need the invigorating shock of experimental art to make the world appear vivid and fresh again. From a Formalist point of view a realistic treatment of the Stalinist era would be inadequate not only because realism was designed to reflect a different order of social and personal existence, but also because, after a century of use, it would fall on deaf ears. That is what may be termed the Formalist basis of Sinyavsky's new artistic credo, though the exact choice of the forms and their elaboration is his own. But this last statement was qualified by Sinyavsky himself when he sketched out the family tree of fantastic realism, a term which, incidentally, owes something to Hoffmann and Dostoevsky, and which a school of contemporary painters in Vienna is using to define their approach to art.

The literature of the fantastic has a few ground rules which must not be transgressed if the illusion (or, rather, the double illusion) is to be sustained. The first rule is that the fantastic premise must be introduced quite early in the narrative, thus taking advantage of the syllogistic workings of the mind whereby deductions are drawn from unquestioned premises. A fantastic element that is introduced too late is disruptive and almost inevitably relegates the story to a lower intellectual and artistic level. Even better, if the narrative opens in rather homely and unprepossessing surroundings, the reader's attention will be firmly caught, then overwhelmed, by the intrusion of another dimension of reality. Gogol's "The Nose" begins in just such a fashion, as do Kafka's "Metamorphosis" and Daniel's "Moscow Speaking." The rational portion of the mind, the as yet unsuspended judgment, must be somehow tricked, astonished, delighted, so that it ceases to function except to judge how logical are the deductions drawn from the original, fantastic premise. An author's finesse is determined by how well he makes the transition from the plane of the real to the plane of the fantastic and how logically and uninterruptedly he draws his deductions, that is, develops his action, once the premise is established and the transition made. After the transition has been made, the relationship between the real and the fantastic should be stabilized, a problem that can be dealt with in more than a single way. There may be a moment in which the entire framework of the narrative is transformed, as in *Alice in Wonderland,* or, as is more usually the case, one element of another dimension may be introduced into the recognizable world, as in "The Nose" or "Metamorphosis." Probably these ground rules or "laws" correspond to some degree to the actual workings of human fantasy, and that is why it is so important for the writer to observe them. His narrative patterns will then be structured in a way that mimics and accords with the workings of fantasy.

Some of the flaws in *The Trial Begins* stem from Sinyavsky's failure to comprehend clearly enough the nature of fantastic fiction. Of course, no aesthetic "law" is so mighty that it cannot be broken by an effort of genius, but, unfortunately, that is not the case here. In the first place, Sinyavsky does not create a satisfactory fantastic premise from which all the subsequent action derives. Fantastic details are introduced before the fantastic premise, thus diminishing its power. For example, we see *s*'s squiggle off the page before the hyperbolic image of Stalin, in the guise of the tyrant-muse of Socialist Realism, orders the narrator to write his book. It cannot be said that all the subsequent action follows from this command in the way that the action in Gogol's "The Nose" follows from the finding of a nose in a loaf of bread, or in Daniel's "Moscow Speaking" from the announcement of Public Murder Day. In fact, though the narrative is very jazzy and uses a great many montage-like effects, the fantastic never cleanly and fully penetrates into the mundane, and the narrative is neither an ideological satire drawn in grotesque caricature style nor a genuine tale of the fantastic, but something in between. All of this renders *The Trial Begins* somewhat disorganized as far as point of view is concerned and does irremediable damage to the tale's structural unity. We are aware of being both dazzled and cheated, and the latter realization brings with it a certain disappointment, an aesthetic letdown. Still, the book has its successes. Sinyavsky's experiment, in which he attempts to incarnate the ideas of *On Socialist Realism* into the artistic vision he announced at the end of that essay, is itself fascinating. Like many failed experiments it can be instructive, and, judging from his later writings, most certainly was for the author himself.

Sinyavsky's intention in *The Trial Begins* is to expose the banality of evil and to make a black comedy out of the ends/means confusion that has bedeviled the Soviet experience. The tale itself is an ingenious mechanism in which relations of the characters are as complicated as an Oscar Wilde plot. The entire complex of relationships forms a political and social allegory most of which anyone familiar with Soviet life would find utterly transparent. This combination of crude satire and obvious allegory produces a grossness inappropriate in a novel of ideas. By 1962 when he finished *The Makepeace Experiment*, Sinyavsky had matured enough as an artist to be able to handle the fantastic premise and to maintain the lightness of tone required by ideological satire if it is not to resemble, in its coarseness, the very coarseness it mocks.

Like *The Makepeace Experiment*, *The Trial Begins* opens with a prologue where the fictional author discusses the origins of the story in which he is both actor and narrator. The device of the first person narrative, which Sinyavsky puts to good use in his subsequent works, in this tale is weak and not fully developed. The narrator, for example, recounts events (dreams within dreams) that could not be known to him and would seem the rightful property of a third person narrator. Two secret police agents, twins, appear at the narrator's apartment, search it, but do not arrest him. They flit throughout the rest of the story, bland, good-natured instruments of evil, a Stalinist version of Gogol's Bobchinsky and Dobchinsky. Sinyavsky's agents undoubtedly owe something to the two characters in *The Trial*, who appear at Joseph K's apartment on his thirtieth birthday.[4] *The Trial Begins* can, of course, be viewed as a Soviet version of *The Trial*, but Sinyavsky does not suffer from the vast metaphysical paranoia of Kafka, and his novel lacks the range and resonance of Kafka's; it is tied to specific events, whereas Kafka's consists entirely of a hallucinatory atmosphere built up gradually, a sentence at a time.

The search is followed by a vision of Stalin as dictator-muse, engineer of the engineers of souls. The narrator is commanded to write the story of Stalin's hero, Vladimir Globov, city public prosecutor. Thus, the prologue satirizes the personality cult, Socialist Realism, and literature by command, and is a continuation of *On Socialist Realism*. Here, as elsewhere in this work, the reader's sensibility plays a crucial role: much of the humor seems labored, the targets too big to miss, the weapon of the satire itself too blunt and crude. But that is a distinctly Western approach in which aesthetic criteria tend to take first place. It is almost impossible to gauge the liberating effect of such literature on Soviet readers, especially younger ones. To refer to Mihajlov once again, the Yugoslavian critic found *The Trial Begins* on a par with *1984* and *The Trial*.

The Trial Begins and Solzhenitsyn's *The First Circle* were among the first novels in Soviet literature to present distinctly negative portraits of Stalin. Their methods, though having much in common, are not identical. Sinyavsky chooses abstraction and buffoonery, mocking Stalin's meddling in literature; the effect of Stalin's life and death on the masses concerns him more than does Stalin's personality. In Sinyavsky's typical ironic and elliptical style, the portrait of Stalin is confined to the opening burlesque, a glimpse from afar, and an aftermath. Solzhenitsyn's treatment is more ambitious, broader, deeper, and more detailed, and though stylized, it still conforms to the canons of realism. Solzhenitsyn too is concerned with tracing the effects of the dictator on Soviet society, but as a connoisseur of human types he is inevitably fascinated with Stalin the man, and devotes four whole chapters of *The First Circle* to him. Although many of Solzhenitsyn's techniques resemble Sinyavsky's, they are more controlled, more realistic, heavy with the sarcasm of a Zek. He too satirizes Stalin's megalomania by parodying the very titles Stalin had created for himself—The Immortal One, Wisest of the Wise, and, finally, Emperor of the Planet. Solzhenitsyn takes a certain pleasure, sweet as revenge, in unmasking the dictator's weakness, terror, and corruption in his nightly bouts with fading memory, paranoia, and the fear of death:

That sensation of fading memory, of failing mind, of loneliness advancing on him like a paralysis, filled him with helpless terror.

Death had already made its nest in him, and he refused to believe it.[5]

Vladimir Globov, the Stalin-appointed hero of *The Trial Begins*, is, like all the rest of the characters, a type with a few individualizing features sketched in. Globov belongs to the ruling elite, the new class, and he and his colleagues are pictured as horrifyingly ordinary. Unlike Solzhenitsyn, Sinyavsky is interested not in moral or psychological nuances but in social types, which he generalizes for both comic and sociological purposes. This class of upper-echelon bureaucrats is described:

These, outwardly, were the coziest of men; their politics were all inside them, deep in their hearts, hidden in the secret place where other mortals keep their vices.

How deluded was the mercenary Western press whose scribblers portrayed these men as somber villains. In reality, they couldn't be nicer; they were witty, home-loving; according to Skromnykh, many of them liked fishing in their spare time, or cooking, or making toys for children. One senior Interrogator, employed on cases of the utmost gravity, used his leisure knitting gloves and embroidering doilies and cushion covers; he maintained that needlework was good for the nervous system.[6]

Globov's second wife, Marina, plays a politically symbolic role much like the one that *On Socialist Realism* ascribes to the heroines of Russian literature. In a society where significant individual action is virtually impossible, the erotic and the political become fused into a single system that illuminates both realms at once. Globov is investigating an illegal abortion performed by a Jewish doctor, not yet realizing that it had been performed on his wife, who refuses to bear him a child; a cold and haughty beauty, concerned only with herself, existing only for herself, Marina is a symbol of the glorious end which justifies any means and which is pursued, in one way or another, by all the characters in the book. Karlinsky, a defense attorney, is a relativist and a cosmopolitan intellectual (the ikon in his room is not in the corner, but next to a Japanese print over the radio) who pursues Marina with unscrupulous passion throughout the novel. Globov is threatened from all sides—Jews are performing illegal abortions (the Doctors' Plot in disguise), his wife is unfaithful and will not bear him a child, and his son Seryozha from his first marriage shows signs of becoming an ideological juvenile delinquent. In a scene playing on the conflict of generations, Globov does his fatherly best to instill in his son that code of moral and political values by which he lives—obedience, dedication to the glorious end, and the belief that civil servants should earn more money than cleaning women. The gulf between the mentalities of father and son is further developed in an account of a concert they attend together. For the father the music is controlled energy, water that can freeze at a signal from the conductor. Globov's is the classical taste of the Soviet bureaucrat and recalls Sinyavsky's remark that the river of art has been frozen over by the ice of classicism.* Their conflict is not only that of two gen-

---

* Similar doubts about Soviet art arose in Eisenstein's mind and took a similar form: "We aren't rebels anymore. We're becoming lazy priests. I have the impression that the enormous breath of 1917 which gave birth to our cinema is blowing itself out. We're getting fat. We're getting classical—'Artistic!'" (From a letter to

erations; it is conflict between the romantic and classical impulses of Soviet literature described in *On Socialist Realism*. Seryozha the son delights in the elemental force of the music, its Blokian, violent, purgative side:

The music reproduced his private image of the Revolution. The flood drowned the whole of the bourgeoisie in a most convincing way.

A general's wife in an evening dress floundered, tried to scramble up a pillar, and was washed away. The old general swam with a vigorous breast stroke but soon sank. . . . Now and then, a bald head, white like an unripe melon, slowly floated up out of the sonorous green depth and bobbed back out of sight.[7]

The father's imagery is of course very different:

The conductor built dams, ditches, aqueducts, canalizing the capricious elements in accordance with his exact blueprint. He directed the flow; at the sweep of his arm one stream froze, another surged forward in its bed and turned a turbine.[8]

Seryozha's attachment to the myth of the Revolution coupled with a child's normal curiosity and idealism leads him into the wilderness of heresy. He becomes the most dangerous enemy of any regime, the man who truly believes in its ideals. His program is a *potpourri* of Trotskyism, radical democracy, naive populism, and the exuberant, revolutionary aesthetics of the twenties:

Leon Moussinac, dated November 22, 1928, Moscow, quoted in Leon Moussinac, *Sergei Eisenstein, An Investigation into His Films and Philosophy* [New York: Crown Publishers, 1970], p. 149.)

Top wages would be paid to cleaningwomen. Cabinet Ministers would be kept on short rations to make sure of their disinterested motives. Money, torture, and thievery would be abolished. Perfect liberty would dawn, and it would be so wonderful that no one would put anyone in jail and everybody would receive according to his needs. The slogans in the streets would be mostly by Mayakovsky; there would also be some by Seryozha, such as "Beware! You might hurt the feelings of your fellow man!" This was just as a reminder, in case people got above themselves. Those who did would be shot.[9]

Like all revolutionaries blinded by idealism, Seryozha is willing to shoot those who stand in the way of the Golden Age. Once again, ends and means are confused. It is not that Sinyavsky has no sympathy for Seryozha's ideas (many of them he seems to share in a less infantile form), but when they coalesce into a system and when someone attempts to put that system into practice, it seems there can be but a single result. Seryozha shares his revolutionary fantasies only with a girl friend, but his grandmother, a typical Russian grandmother with a revolutionary overlay, is somewhat responsible for his heretical enthusiasms. She pretends to be very hard-boiled and marks the progress of the Korean War with little red flags on her map. The grandmotherly and the political are comically mixed in her: "At your age we were all in jail. Want something to eat?" [10] When Seryozha is arrested, her human loyalties outweigh her political ones. Tikhomirov's mother in *The Makepeace Experiment* is a similar figure and plays the same sort of sane, corrective role.

The most interesting and carefully drawn character in

The Trial Begins is Yuri Karlinsky, the defense counselor. To identify him with the author would be incorrect even though many of Karlinsky's private thoughts on death, sex, and faith reappear as aphorisms in the collection *Thought Unaware*. Karlinsky is a sophisticated intellectual who professes a sort of cynical relativism and is haunted by insomnia, the fear of death, and the inability to find faith or meaning in life. A typical modern Soviet intellectual, he has no faith in Marxist philosophy, his critical intelligence keeps him from being absorbed into the bureaucratic elite, and yet he is unable to commit himself to those ethical and spiritual values which were the traditional concerns of the prerevolutionary intelligentsia and remain the concern of its small, post-Stalin counterpart. He has no illusions on this score and mocks himself accordingly: "But what had *he* to offer the world in his own name? Some pot-pourri of Freud and a Hawaiian guitar?" [11] Andrei Amalrik was speaking about a similar fetishism of the West when he wrote about freedom in his open letter to Anatoli Kuznetsov upon the latter's defection to the West:

You speak all the time of freedom, but of external freedom, the freedom around us, and you say nothing of the inner freedom, that is, the freedom according to which the authorities can do much to a man but by which they are powerless to deprive him of his moral values.[12]

It is precisely this inner freedom that the best of the contemporary Soviet intelligentsia have developed (and which we can observe developing in Sinyavsky by watching the evolution of his art) as a bastion against tyranny from without, and of which Karlinsky is incapable. Perhaps the portrait of Karlinsky contains traces of the autobiographical, depicting Sinyavsky in his moments of despair between one faith and another, or perhaps he represents what Sinyavsky feared becoming. In a more general sense, Karlinsky may be viewed as a representative of the intelligentsia in the fifties before the resistance movement had gathered momentum. The contemplation of death and the realization that its certainty makes life cruel and absurd draw him to the brink of spiritual crisis: for Sinyavsky, however, the thought of death is always accompanied by a sense of liberation, of being freed by contact with the eternal, the natural, the inevitable, from the mundane and historical. Karlinsky's solution is not Sinyavsky's:

Self-deception was the only way out. This was the remedy in common use, anything to take your mind off this nothingness, which could easily drive you mad. Some went in for politics, like that oaf Globov. Others, like Marina escaped into . . . Marina! And here—here surely was his salvation! . . . Let Marina be his fulcrum. Marina, the inaccessible, who thought herself the sole end of creation, would be the means of curing his insomnia. As for the end—the end would be himself, Yury, —and Yury's victory over Marina.[13]

In a curiously Western manner Karlinsky tries to fill the metaphysical void with sexual activity. Though the book contains some real enough erotic moments, its treatment of the erotic should not be taken entirely literally, for the Karlinsky-Marina relationship is actually a translation into fictional form of Sinyavsky's ideas about the spiritual hunger of the intelligentsia and the politically symbolic role of women in Russian literature.[14]

Karlinsky courts Marina in restaurants, museums, and a planetarium. The scene in the planetarium, like the description of the soccer match, is much in debt to Olesha's *Envy*. Both writers are concerned with the "new man," his vulgarity, and the dangers he represents, but Olesha, writing before the advent of Stalinism, is more Chaplinesque and fanciful than Sinyavsky, who is as pitiless toward his superfluous man as he is to members of the establishment. The description of the planetarium ceiling is straight Olesha:

> In the vaulted ceiling overhead, the starry heavens were switched on. The universe hung above them, with its billions of stars turning slowly with a slight creak of hinges, just as in a real sky. It revealed its depths, tumbled out the contents, and showed for certain that there was no God.[15]

Like Olesha, Sinyavsky mocks the artificial stars chosen by Soviet lovers, but goes him one better. He jibes at the confusing of the scientific model of the universe with the universe itself, and at the erroneous conclusions drawn from that mixup.

The role that Karlinsky plays in the unfolding of the plot is crucial: he destroys the hopes of Seryozha's confidante Katya, and later he turns in Seryozha to clear his path to Marina. The passage in which he annihilates the childish program of Seryozha and Katya is a parody on language gone berserk in the mind of an intellectual who has said the same words so often without conviction that they have been worn down into meaningless stumps of prefixes and suffixes:

Counter . . . xism . . . ism, ism, ism . . .
Principle . . . incible . . .
Jective . . .
Manity . . . lution . . . *Pferd* . . .[16]

Sinyavsky puts the explicit theme of the novel into the mouth of Rabinovich, the Jewish doctor who performs the abortion on Marina, thus robbing Globov of his longed-for daughter. During a feverish, multidimensional dream Rabinovich says: "Every decent End consumes itself. You kill yourself trying to reach it, and by the time you get there it's been turned inside out." [17] This is the message of the novel, the theme that each of the characters lives out, which culminates in Globov's madness, Marina's barrenness, and Karlinsky's impotence. Karlinsky's impotence proves that the end does not justify the means, that the material of life ultimately will rebel against being driven toward goals that violate its nature. The body, like Seryozha's grandmother, represents an elemental sanity that refuses to assent to the delusions of the mind. Here we see the beginning of the way out for Sinyavsky. Rather than seeking out a new program, a new preformulated vision, he will explore and praise the variety and mystery of life, not in the panegyric fashion of Pasternak, but always with a trace of irony, a sense of rootedness in the world. All of the characters in *The Trial Begins* are punished and all are equally callous—Karlinsky betrays Seryozha, Globov disowns him, and Marina is perfectly indifferent to her aborted child. The general utilitarian callousness of Soviet society is capsulized in the suggestion, after Jonathan Swift, of turning human embryos into food, thus once and for all solving the Malthusian dilemma.

Stalin ("The Master") appears three times in *The Trial Begins*—once as muse-dictator, once at the barely visible object of adoration by a surging mob, and finally as a negative presence, the dead Master who has abandoned his people. Though Stalin ordered the narrator to make Globov the hero of the work, the narrator, willy-nilly, focuses on the illnesses of the collective. Later in the narrative he confesses that the book is being written, not from positive motives, but out of dread. The following passage, containing an echo of the role played by the arrest of his father in Sinyavsky's development as a writer, contains an uneasy, prophetic note about Sinyavsky's own probable fate:

The Court is in session, it is in session throughout the world. And not only Rabinovich, unmasked by the City Prosecutor, but all of us, however many we may be, are daily, nightly, tried and questioned. This is called history.

The doorbell rings. Surname? Christian name? Date of birth? This is when you begin to write.[18]

The two other passages dealing with Stalin show him in relation to the collective. The crowd is depicted going into frenzies over a distant dot which may or may not be Stalin. Only Seryozha, like the little boy who noticed the Emperor was naked, cannot see Stalin. The scene of Stalin's funeral is a companion piece to the crowd scene. Both scenes examine the behavioral psychology of the collective, its need and ability to worship a leader, and the sense of desolation that the leader's death produces. The crowd bereft of its leader is compared to a dog whose master has died:

> The Master was dead.
>
> The town seemed empty as a desert. You felt like sitting on your haunches, lifting up your head, and howling like a homeless dog. . . .
> Already, you can hear a whine here and there:
> "Let's live in freedom and enjoy ourselves, like wolves."
> But I know, I know only too well, how they guzzled in the past, these mercenary creatures—poodles, spaniels, pugs. And I don't want freedom. I want a Master.[19]

The word "khozyain" (Master) used by Sinyavsky in the original makes the reference to Stalin explicit, for "khozyain" was the most common way of referring to him.

Amalrik has expressed a similar opinion concerning the Russians' relation to freedom: "To the majority of the people the very word 'freedom' is synonymous with 'disorder' or the opportunity to indulge with impunity in some kind of antisocial or dangerous activity."[20]

For Russians especially the question of freedom has never been a simple one. Before the abolition of serfdom in 1861, a common rationalization for its preservation was that without it the people would run wild. Thus a vicious circle was established—the people need to be free and yet, having lived so long without freedom, would not know how to react if suddenly freed. Of course, the waters are further muddied by the attraction/repulsion the intelligentsia has traditionally felt for the people. For the intellectuals of the post-Stalin period, the meaning of freedom is the central question, but it remains a problematic one. Amalrik, very much a Westerner in outlook, takes a pessimistic view of the Russian people, based on observations made during his years of banishment for being a "parasite," and elaborated in his book *Involuntary Journey to Siberia*. Sinyavsky, though in his work as a teacher and critic he pushes for greater freedom, nevertheless retains a mystic's scepticism about freedom. Freedom for what? And in the end he decides—freedom to give yourself to the thing of your own choosing, to be yourself. For some it is a question of new or reformed institutions, of living up to the Soviet constitution, whereas others seem to simply desire an atmosphere of freedom and respect for the individual, to be left alone by the authorities so that life can go its own way. Profound scepticism would have to be given first place in any characterization of the Soviet dissident, scepticism toward all philosophical and political systems, for such total systems are traps for free minds and can too easily become the rationale for prisons. Thus, the scepticism of the dissidents is neither negative nor sterile but a healthy response to malignant dogmatism and repression.

Sinyavsky is clearly a descendant of Gogol, Remizov, and Bely, for whom the verbal texture of a work is of equal or near equal importance to the workings of the plot, and from the onset of his career Sinyavsky is most successful and brilliant on the verbal level. He is acutely sensitive to all the linguistic strata of contemporary Russian from slang to official doubletalk. This intimate grasp of modern Russian speech led some critics to believe that the works of Tertz could not be forgeries or hoaxes written by a Russian living abroad. But it is not only the variety and color of language that interest Sinyavsky, but the attempt to regenerate his native language distorted by years of propaganda and doublethink. In an article entitled "The New Idiom," Leonid Rzhevsky makes a case for the stylistic experiments of the new writers as a form of creative opposition to the officialese of the establishment: "It is precisely the 'poor quality' of the language used by organs of the central and provincial press, its poverty, the ugliness of its stilted bureaucratic jargon, the monotony of its officialese and rigid cliches, that is directly or indirectly attacked by the stylistic purists." [21]

Tone, the elusive essence of all fiction, present in every syllable and constantly changing, is the element closest to an author, to his relation to his work. Some works that describe horrible and discordant events are nevertheless pervaded by a sense of harmony, whereas others, though placid and serene, produce a troubling response in the reader; the inner life of an author is much more intimately related to the subtlest and purest aesthetic qualities of a work than to any autobiographical details he may knowingly or unknowingly have included. Listening closely to the tone of *The Trial Begins*, we find it restless, erratic, not flowing from a single, stable center, reflecting the author's difficulty in finding a unified relationship to his fable, and reflecting as well perhaps the fertile chaos of the year 1956. The satire proceeds not so much from a sense of disparity between what things could be and what they actually are, as from a sense of what they were advertised to be and what they in fact are. In other words the satire is rooted in his disenchantment, not in his own vision of life. In *The Makepeace Experiment*, Sinyavsky's last work to reach the West before his arrest, many of the same elements are present, but there they are united by a personal vision and purged of sarcasm and hostility.

5

Solitaria

> "Man"—that rings proud.
>
> Gorky
>
> Enough affirming man.
> Time to think of God a while.
>
> Sinyavsky

Thought Unaware belongs to both aphoristic and confessional literature. It has its place beside Baudelaire's *My Heart Laid Bare* and Rousseau's *Confessions,* but it is a very Russian work, richly imbued with the metaphysical spirit of the Silver Age in general and with the personality and style of the Silver Age aphorist Vasily Rozanov in particular. The problems of such literature are well known—vanity, straight or inverse, is the Heisenberg factor in all examinations of the self, and the following exchange from Sinyavsky's trial should be interpreted in that light:

Judge: All those "unguarded thoughts" of yours—is that the author speaking?
Sinyavsky: Not entirely. (*laughter in the courtroom*) [1]

Sinyavsky was of course referring to the difficulty of being honest, even in private, let alone in a Soviet court room, and also to the fact that *Thought Unaware* is not a purely random sampling of thoughts but an artistic work, an orchestrated score of aphorisms in which the thoughts are notes, chords, and themes. We should not be deceived by the title, which speaks of the nature of thinking and intuition, its sudden, unexpected intrusion into consciousness, and not of the composition of the work itself. This work also represents a continuation of the search for new forms of creative expression which Sinyavsky announced at the end of *On Socialist Realism* and first put into practice in *The Trial Begins*. Whereas the latter is an intellectually structured artistic work, his aphorisms are an artistically structured intellectual work.

Thought Unaware must be viewed as carrying on the effort of the nineteenth-century Romantics to blur the distinctions between literary genres for the purpose of liberating expression from forms no longer considered sufficiently flexible to absorb and project the spirit of the age or the style of a man. Byron's "Beppo," Pushkin's *Yevgeny Onegin*, and the modern documentary novel, or novel of fact, such as Capote's *In Cold Blood* or Anatoli Kuznetsov's *Babi Yar*, are all examples of the tendency to create new forms by merging those traditionally kept separate. The point here is that Sinyavsky, when he gives his inner autobiography an artistic form, is taking a form and putting it to new use. Most previous collections of aphorisms were either, like Rozanov's, a random sampling of thoughts and remarks or, like Nietzsche's, a series of thoughts arranged in a consistently logical pattern to prove a point or show the crystallization of a mental attitude. Sinyavsky violates those assumptions on the one hand by eschewing randomness, and on the other, by arranging his ideas in a nonlogical sequence so that they provide the same sort of aesthetic pleasure as poetry or music.

The aphorism has recently fallen into disfavor, perhaps because it is considered too genteel for an age of barbarism and scientific miracles, perhaps because men no longer feel they have the authority, the clarity, to make unambiguous pronouncements about the nature of the things in the manner of Goethe or Samuel Johnson. Sinyavsky circumvents in part the contemporary objection to aphorisms by refusing to make unambiguous statements—his collection of aphorisms may be read as statements in which the author allows his obsessions and attitudes to rise naturally to the surface, without attempting anything definitive. The aphorism as a convenient means of expressing a personal, subjective reaction to existence fits in very nicely with Sinyavsky's need to find his own vantage point and with his basic scepticism. It is a literary form at once precise and romantic and thus very much in keeping with Sinyavsky's nature.

Under the specific conditions of Soviet cultural politics, the form itself of the aphorism has something heretical and rebellious about it. If the novel is the Soviet art form *par excellence* because it necessarily treats of the collective, then the aphorism must be evidence of a renegade concern with personal existence, apart from the collective, apart from history, apart from Purpose. Sinyavsky is well aware of this, and his principal themes—death, sex, faith—are

treated not as a superstructure, but as inescapably private
concerns which, by their nature, shift a man's awareness
from the social plane to the private and the cosmic, and
thus permit him to develop a fuller sense of his own life,
individuality, and nature.

To the best of my knowledge, only one writer in the
communist world has experimented with the aphorism, and
a comparison of his style with Sinyavsky's will show the
peculiarly Russian and peculiarly Sinyavskian elements in
Thought Unaware. That other aphorist is a Pole, Stanisław
Lec, who died in 1969. His aphorisms appeared in two separate collections, each entitled *Unkempt Thoughts* (*Mysli
Nieuczesane*), a title close enough to Sinyavsky's to suggest
deliberate echoing. At first glance, the two writers appear
to be somewhat alike—both are masters of irony and both
mix fun and despair with that bittersweet sagacity peculiar
to Eastern Europe. There is, of course, the obvious difference that Lec's aphorisms are for the most part one-liners,
"uncombed" into any order. Let us look at a few of Lec's
aphorisms:

Don't tell your dreams. What if the Freudists come to power?

Is it progress if a cannibal uses a knife and fork?

To God what is God's, to Caesar what is Caesar's. To humans
—what? [2]

Like the most significant Polish poets of the post-Stalin
period, Zbigniew Herbert and Tadeusz Różewicz, Lec saw
social and historical events as points of intersection be-

tween personal life and the superhuman forces of nature
and time. Herbert, for example, was able to translate the
Hamlet image into social terms in his "Elegy of Fortin-
bras" or to merge the Last Judgment and a death camp in
"At the Gates of the Valley" without diminishing the
power of the original images; quite the reverse, using the
images in a new context recharges them, and, correspond-
ingly, illuminates their sources. Of course, having the personal and the metaphysical intersect on the historical plane
was exactly what Sinyavsky was attempting in *The Trial
Begins* and achieved later on with greater success in *The
Makepeace Experiment*. But in *Thought Unaware*, Sinyavsky's intention is quite different: he is trying to create
some breathing space for himself, a little corner away from
his society, his conditioning, his age, and though he speaks
of matters that are somewhat impersonal, such as the church
and the Russian people, they appear as a portion of his vision, connected with its other themes, and not as detached
objects for reflection.

   The need to escape from the temporal to the eternal gave
rise to the Silver Age in Russian literature and culture, and
it is to the literature of that age that Sinyavsky turns for
models, inspiration, and refuge. The Silver Age, one of
Sinyavsky's areas of specialization as a literary critic, was
a fertile and complex period in Russian history whose
nature and implications have still to be fully traced. During
this time, at the end of the nineteenth century and in the
first two decades of the twentieth, poetry, after a long
dormancy, suddenly blossomed to life again, and philosophy

enlarged its perspective by treating the temporal world as a reflection of the eternal. This metaphysical flowering on the eve of social upheaval provides a model for the relationship between culture and history in a period of great stress, and a possible source of valuable analogies for contemporary and future historians. The concern of Berdyaev and other Silver Age philosophers with inner freedom seems very close to that of Solzhenitsyn and Sinyavsky, but with a certain difference. For the former, inner freedom was a bastion against the coming inundation, whereas for the latter it is a means of self-defense against the machinations of the system. Still, they have all withdrawn to the same solitary contemplative point in an effort to stabilize themselves in the face of overpowering events.

In *Thought Unaware* Sinyavsky draws upon and pays homage to one of the almost forgotten men of Russian literature, Vasily Rozanov. Rozanov (1856–1919) is nearly an unperson in the Soviet Union, and the only official source of information about him is a few niggardly, disparaging lines in the Soviet Encylopedia. None of his works is available in book stores, but literary specialists have obviously had access to them. He is quoted by Sinyavsky in his critical study *The Poetry of the First Years of the Revolution,* and also by Mihajlov in his study of Sinyavsky-Tertz, *Escape from the Test Tube.* In his book *Moscow Summer,* Mihajlov recounts his conversations with Shklovsky about Rozanov and another Silver Age metaphysician, Vladimir Solovev. So Rozanov has never been really forgotten in Russia or by Russians living abroad; like Solovev, he seems to have become something of an underground culture hero in the Soviet Union for a certain segment of the contemporary intelligentsia. But his reemergence in the aphorisms of a young Soviet writer must be a first of its kind.

Although his unsavory anti-Semitism (made even more unsavory by his equally genuine fondness for Jewish culture and the Old Testament) and his historically premature open fascination with sexuality made Rozanov a *persona non grata* to both the Soviets and the émigrés, he was too great a genius, albeit a cranky, unpleasant one, and too interesting a writer ever to disappear completely. Not only has he resurfaced in Sinyavsky's aphorisms, but the émigrés have begun republishing and reevaluating his works. His aphoristic collections, *Solitaria, Fallen Leaves I,* and *Fallen Leaves II,* were random thoughts jotted down sometimes on scraps of paper and once even on the sole of his slipper while he was taking a bath; they were written in the form in which they had appeared in the author's mind, and never reworked, for Rozanov delighted in the gratuitous, organic process of thought. There are themes running through all these aphorisms, but they are just Rozanov's preocupations, fears, daily and spiritual concerns, and there has been no attempt to structure them into patterns. The author himself referred to the collections as "bushels" or "baskets" to contain his "fallen leaves." For Rozanov thinking was a biological process, ideas were organic events that took place in the mental or psychological zone. Gippius, Berdyaev, and others have praised him for his style of writing, which some consider nearly perfect because there is no apparent gap between the intention and the execution.

Rozanov prefaces *Solitaria* with a description of its origin:

The wind blows at midnight and carries away leaves. . . . So also life in fleeting time tears off from our soul exclamations, sighs, half-thoughts, half-feelings . . . which, being fragments of sound, have the significance that they "come" straight from the soul, without elaboration, without purpose, without premeditation—without anything external. Simply, "the soul is alive," that is, "has lived," "has breathed." [3]

Sinyavsky begins, and closes his *Thought Unaware* with aphorisms on the thought process that echo Rozanov's sentiments:

You can live like a perfect fool, and still magnificent thoughts will sometimes begin to creep into your head. [4]

One's thoughts stop and cease to come as soon as one begins to collect and consider them. [5]

In introducing their aphorisms both authors stress the spontaneity of their thoughts and feelings, and Rozanov underscores the fact that his aphorisms are useful only to himself. In both writers, one feels a conscious, spiritual rebellion against the dictates of time and place and against the imperative to make thought socially useful. There are also many similarities in the style of the two writers. Both delight in discussing lofty matters in ordinary, homely, even vulgar language, thus stressing the intimate connection between high and low, grand and trivial. Rozanov uses the highly colloquial and elliptic language of everyday speech with a little of the kitschiness and *Gemütlichkeit* of the Russian petit bourgeois thrown in, whereas Sinyavsky draws on Soviet jargon and slang, and his intonations are more worldly-wise, urban, and hip than Rozanov's. Both use punctuation expressively to suggest the natural contours of speech or thought, especially three dots at the end of a phrase to suggest a thought trailing back into the nothingness from which it arose. Their obsessions too are nearly identical—sex, death, faith, the nature and destiny of the Russian people. It is in their open fascination with sexuality that these writers are especially close. But they have points of divergence, the two main ones being what might be called their spiritual style and their attitude toward sexuality.

Compared with Sinyavsky, Rozanov seems almost totally devoid of humor. All his life he strove, not for the distance from self that is the prerequisite of humor, but for utter self-immersion in the organic flow of existence, mental existence as well as physical. Rozanov treats his thoughts as pure, spontaneous phenomena of which he is conscious but over which he has no control. He witnesses them as he would witness a shooting star or a falling leaf. Sinyavsky, on the other hand, leavens his musings with jokes, irony, and sarcasm, usually at his own expense, as in those Yiddish tales and proverbs which are at once a revelation and a joke. That "Jewish" side of Sinyavsky is caught by Wat, who sees in him "Jewish *Mutterwitz* as well as truly Muscovite sarcasm, and Jewish hysteria side by side with *muzhik* coarseness." [6] Sinyavsky's first novel deals with the anti-Semitic Doctors' Plot, and his pseudonym, Abram Tertz, is, especially to Russian ears, distinctly Jewish. Jews hold a certain fascination for Sinyavsky, as they did for Rozanov, but Sinyavsky's attitude toward them is altogether more sane and healthy; it will be discussed in greater detail in Chapter 7, "History versus the People." As far as his self-mocking humor is concerned, at his trial Sinyavsky agreed "up to a point" with the definition of *Thought Unaware* as "self-flagellation in front of a mirror."

Sinyavsky's and Rozanov's philosophies diverge on the question of sex. Rozanov's principal intuition—the unity of flesh and spirit, not materialism, but divine biology—was ahead of its time, and prompted D. H. Lawrence to say of Rozanov that he "mattered, for the future." [7] Sinyavsky on the other hand, suffers and enjoys the traditional spirit/ flesh dichotomy and thus, in comparison with Rozanov, appears something of a throwback. For Sinyavsky shame is a virtue and a proof of the human ascendancy over the animals, for shame results from a spiritual perception of the conflict between spirit and flesh, whereas Rozanov thought it a mere aberration, or proof of the numinous quality of sexuality. Andrew Field sums up this difference very neatly when he writes in the introduction to *Thought Unaware:* "Rozanov viewed sex as the key to the divine, as opposed to Tertz-Sinyavsky who sees it as the padlock." [8] This statement should not be taken to mean that Sinyavsky has a simple aversion for sex: his attitude is much more complicated and interesting than that, and to Western eyes, after a decade of liberated libido, it seems almost exotic. The problem is not that Sinyavsky is so much repelled by sex as that he is both strongly repelled and attracted by it. In fact, there is a sort of secondary repulsion for him—repulsion at being so attracted. But his concern is not only with his own and man's sexual nature, but with the physicality of existence as well. He is both horrified and amused by the filth that man, alone among all animals, continually produces:

Somehow filth and trash converge around man. . . . The last dropping is the body of the deceased which also demands that it be carried away as quickly as possible.[9]

Like George Bernard Shaw, Sinyavsky views the proximity of the sexual and excretory organs as "God's irony";

The very location of our sex is fatal—in immediate proximity to the organs of excretion. It's as though a disgusted, sarcastic grimace were provided by nature itself.[10]

This passage recalls Berdyaev's confession of "fastidiousness" in his autobiography, and his quoting Leonardo da Vinci to the effect that the human genitals are so ugly that human beings must be seized by a form of madness in order to copulate. Though he calls the sexual act "a feast in a cesspool" (*pir v kloske*), Sinyavsky can hardly be viewed as abstinent if we can credit the following aphorism of his:

I was her 67th, she was my 45th.[11]

Few verbal gestures are as indicative as comic ones of the psychology behind them, and it is worth considering for a moment a few of the implications of this one-line aphorism-joke made at the author's own expense. It contains in essence several of the attitudes Sinyavsky develops at greater length in other aphorisms. The humor comes from the numbers, their precision (one is not expected to be so cut and dried in such matters), their size, by which the author seems to be indicating his whimsical helplessness against the sexual urge, and perhaps from the fact that the woman is considerably more experienced than he. Sex has not filled the void as Lawrence and Rozanov and the other sexual Romantics believed it would, but like any other natural appetite it keeps on recurring with utter disregard for the morality or philosophy of its host. That is why Sinyavsky views it as an obstacle to inner freedom and why, in the end, he exclaims, half in earnest, half in jest:

Oh to become a eunuch—how much you could get accomplished! [12]

What concerns Sinyavsky is the dark side of sexuality. His resentment of its power over the will and soul is used for symbolic ends in *The Trial Begins* and burlesqued marvelously and point-blank in "Phentz." In this respect Sinyavsky is close to Tolstoy, in one of whose stories a horse named Kholstomer is able to reach a philosophic view of life only after he has been gelded; another story by Tolstoy from the same period, "The Devil," studies the damage wrought by uncontrollable desire and is marked by the same animosity toward the sex drive, not a fear of the act but a resentment of the power of its demand. The psychopathology of desire interests Sinyavsky as well:

In sexual relations there is something pathological. . . . In the sex act there is always present something of the Black Mass.[13]

The magical transformation of an ordinary woman, who was was once a little girl and is destined to be a grandmother, into a creature capable of bewitching a man, of inciting so much desire in him that he loses control of himself and sight of his goals, fascinates Sinyavsky. The process of attraction is marked by a sudden increase in energy, a sense of power lost or power gained (the choice of the term "black mass" is apt because the devil signifies power, not love—domination, not equality).

Unlike the sexual reformers and the Romantics, Sinyavsky views sexuality as shameful. Shame he considers good and proper because it proceeds not only from the ugliness of the human body but from a sense of sin and fall from grace (*grekhopadenie*). The myth of the Fall of Man is central to Sinyavsky's thinking and to his relation to the world; it posits a higher order of values to which man by his nature and origin belongs, but from which he has departed. The Fall of Man is the beginning of history, and Sinyavsky in his attempt to struggle free from the domination of history, sees historical man as fallen man in his continuing Fall; thus he views man in reference to a scale of values which are not historically determined, but spiritual, preexisting, eternal, in a sense "outside" of man, and to which man is connected by his mortality and his imagination.

The sexual themes which recur in Sinyavsky's writings are not to be identified in the cruder sense of that word with the author, that is, they are, of course, his problems, but not *his* problem. In fact, the sexual theme is not isolated from the rest of his personality and his search for self-definition; rather, it is simply one variation of it, one manifestation. It is dangerous and irresponsible to drop a phrase like "latent homosexuality," as did one critic, without further elaboration—this is watered-down Freudianism of the worst sort, and the effort to identify a man with a neurosis is simple tyranny, a trick that has not been overlooked by the Soviet regime. Further, it should be remembered that Sinyavsky is treating themes which he has already defined as containing both personal and social implications, and since he follows his own prescription and mixes political and erotic symbols, one must be very cautious in abstracting specific conclusions. In fact, only lately have psychiatrists begun to realize that individual problems may be related to collective illnesses just as well as to neuroses and traumas. In a society which severely restricts individual initiative, there is bound to be some reflection of the resulting frustration in the individual and his relations with other human beings.

The Soviet writers' lack of exposure to the latest experiments of European and American fiction is not without its healthy side. What Western authors began as an investigation of the subleties of individual psychology has sometimes degenerated into sensationalism and pornography. Sinyav-

sky's art is social, philosophical, satirical; his concern is
subjective consciousness, not the dark and ugly little secrets
of the unconscious, and for that reason, as I have already
remarked, his style should be called fantastic realism rather
than surrealism.

For Sinyavsky, the great measures, death and eternity,
turn human vanities into jokes by placing them in their
proper perspective, as the following aphorism clearly
illustrates:

Picture a genius in the next world. He runs from corner to
corner—in Hell—and proves to everyone: But listen, me, I've
got talent! [14]

But Sinyavsky does not joke about death itself; of God and
death he speaks reverently, joyously, with an intimacy that
borders on familiarity, which again brings him close to
Rozanov:

Abraham was called by God. In my case God was called by
me. . . . That's the whole difference.[15]

Death is the one spiritual experience that, in Sinyavsky's
view, society and technology have not yet stolen from man
(though death has been done away with in a work
of Soviet science fiction, *Notes from the Future*, by
N. Amosov). The sacraments may be prohibited or meaningless and all the events of daily life thoroughly secularized,
but death and dying still belong to the individual man and
thereby prove his ultimate relationship to a world vaster
than the human. Sinyavsky's preoccupation with death is
not morbid; on the contrary it is fearless and confident:

One should die exclaiming (whispering) before death: "Hurray, we're sailing off!" [16]

Death is a thrilling adventure, an inescapable encounter with oneself and with ultimate reality (an experience which may occur at any time in one's life but which also may be avoided until the last minute as Tolstoy has described in "The Death of Ivan Ilyich"). The very first aphorism after the opening one on the nature of thought attacks the fear of death and concludes:

Look here—stop trembling! Put a smile on your face! Forward march! [17]

Sinyavsky rebels against Humanism in the name of man and God. Since the Renaissance, man has been making over the world in his own image until now, in the twentieth century, it has become alien and unrecognizably inhuman. Death is the only crack in the Soviet world-view, the only aperture through which Sinyavsky can inhale a breath of the infinite. His contemporary, the poet Yevgeny Vinokurov, expresses an identical notion:

> And in a world where all is boundary,
> everything just barrier and limit,
> fathomless infinity, you
> are my only consolation!
> A crack in some barn wall
> a strip of shining blue—
> and there's the proof that in this world
> not everything's so flat and drab.[18]

Death was the only crack in Rozanov's world-view as well, but for him its significance was decidedly negative.

Rozanov could see no divinity, no meaning outside the warm, biological flow of life, and, with his penchant for physicalizing everything, he referred to death as "the grave" and trembled before its coldness. Death made something of a mockery of his anti-Christian philosophy, for whenever the dread of the grave was upon him, he scurried back into the warm embrace of the church. Neither as a man nor as a thinker did Rozanov possess a stable center (his lack of judgment and conscience combined with his talent and feeling is what makes him so intriguing). The prophet of holy biology could write:

A man achieves genuine seriousness only when dying.
Can it really be that all of life is frivolousness?
All of it.[19]

Though Rozanov's philosophy was not, strictly speaking, materialistic, it shared a weakness of materialism—it was unable to integrate death into a system of meaning. For Sinyavsky death is not a random, meaningless, cruel annihilation but a natural consummation, a blessing, and a goal:

Probably death (even as a simple physical disappearance), like everything else in this world, has to be earned.[20]

Death is the end (in both the literal and philosophical sense of the word) of each human life, and it has to seem hostile to those who live a life without any reference to or connection with the universal, the spiritual, that which is greater than man. Placing a quotation from Sinyavsky alongside one from Jung, we are struck by the concordance of the views of these dissimilar men living in very dissimilar conditions:

Man lives in order to die. . . . It is the logical conclusion to which one comes by the path of life's proof, not a break but a finale, long in preparation, beginning from birth.[21]

And Jung:

As the arrow flies to the target, so life ends in death, which is the target of all life. Even the ascent and its climax are but steps and means to the end, to reach the target, death.[22]

Sinyavsky seeks some leverage for the spirit outside of society, conditioning, environment, just as Dostoevsky had: Dostoevsky found it in man's irrationality, and here Sinyavsky finds it in man's mortality. In *On Socialist Realism* Sinyavsky lampoons Marxism for its cosmic provincialism, which declares that the physical universe exists so that communism may arise dialectically out of the historical processes of planet Earth. Other people in the socialist countries of Eastern Europe share Sinyavsky's sense of Marxism's limitations, and the works of Teilhard de Chardin, who has attempted to spiritualize history and evolution by viewing them as manifestations of God in time, now enjoy considerable popularity in these countries. But Sinyavsky himself has no interest in grand schemes or genial syntheses which explain everything: in his solitary, contemplative hours he draws nearer to the mystery of the soul by fixing his attention on the mystery of death.

Waiting for the end of my life, I managed to accomplish a great deal. Oh how slow is the approach of death! [23]

This aphorism has a true, hair-raising metaphysical ring to it. Whereas, according to Sinyavsky, sexuality binds men to the world of vanity, power, falseness, the contemplation of death, like death itself, liberates men from that world:

Death separates the soul from the body as a butcher separates meat from bone. And it's just as torturous. But that's the only way liberation comes.[24]

Sinyavsky does not just cogitate about God; like a character from the Old Testament he relates to Him, addresses Him. Principally, he addresses God in an effort to recover a spiritual, suprahuman basis for his life. All the disciplines which modern man has created inundate him with information about himself, and yet they seem to have led not to greater clarity but to deeper confusion. The information they supply does not describe man's ultimate nature but only his behavior and environment. Just as the truth of life is illuminated by death, the truth of man is to be sought in God, that is, "outside":

We've had enough affirmations of Man. It's time to think about God.[25]

For Sinyavsky God is self-evident:

One must believe for this reason—God exists.[26]

The laws of nature are a miracle extending through time and space.[27]

These are not isolated statements—they are themes whose meaning can be fully grasped only if they are read in conjunction with the other aphorisms. For example, the following selection is best understood in the light of the previously quoted aphorism on nature as a miracle.

My fuses had all burnt out. I was very depressed, considered myself lost, and asked God for help. And God sent me an Electrician. And the Electrician fixed my fuses.[28]

Here, as in Rozanov, tone is all. On another man's lips this well might sound like antireligious sarcasm, a belittlement of the religious explanations of mundane phenomena which always have something childish about them, but in fact it is a homely, metaphysical joke, with the comedy being born from the tension of opposites, the sublime and trivial, the divine and the quotidian. The aphorism is funny precisely because the author is in earnest. The theme appears again when Sinyavsky wistfully implores God for a miracle, nothing dramatic, just a rather minor miracle:

I don't ask a miracle, just some kind of barely perceptible signal. Let, say, a bug fly out of that bush . . .[29]

Again the joke is at Sinyavsky's expense: even though he believes in God, simply because God is, he would still like a little sign that God is aware of Sinyavsky.

When he speaks of the Russian people, Sinyavsky leans in two directions at once—toward the tradition of caustic disparagement initiated by Chaadaev, and toward the Slavophile tradition that tends to see virtue in vice, strength in weakness. The general line of the Chaadaev tradition maintains that it is impossible for Russians to create a real society, a genuine, organic culture and history, because they have failed to internalize the values of civilization and prefer the formlessness of spontaneous human relations and impulse to strict forms of etiquette, roles, and other devices for modulating and shaping social behavior. For Sinyavsky, who has Christian anarchist as well as Slavophile tendencies, this absence of form is not at all a bad thing—he is rebelling against the superimposition of form whether in literature or politics, feeling or thought. The historical immaturity of the Russians, their lack of an internalized sense of social responsibility Sinyavsky connects to the national habit, tradition, vice, of drinking vodka, which he terms "white magic" and finds preferable to the somehow foreign, un-Russian "black magic" of sexuality. Vodka leads to ecstasy, to religious consciousness ("the Russian drinks, if you please, mystically"). The preference is not for the well-ordered, harmoniously developing society but for the moment of rapture, and liberation, a kinship for the life-giving irrational which Dostoevsky saw as a hint of man's divine origin. Sinyavsky views Russian history as a struggle between those who impose order from above and those who either passively accept that order or reject it with irrational passion: the image he chooses is that of a policeman having to deal with a drunkard:

It's easy to order us about, to direct us by administrative measures (a drunkard is inert, incapable of self-direction, he drags along in the direction he's pulled). And one should also keep in mind how difficult it is to rule this wavering people, how oppressive this rule is for our administrators! [30]

Compared with Amalrik's almost unmitigated scorn of the mass of the Russian people, Sinyavsky's attitude is more in the love/hate tradition of Lermontov, Blok, Rozanov, and others, but his tolerant and affectionate humor is free of that excessive gravity that Russians reserve for the "cursed questions." In the end, Sinyavsky leans toward the conclusions of Chaadaev, who thought that Russia would never have an authentic history and exists solely to teach the world some great lessons, then to vanish:

We are capable of putting Europe in our pocket or of loosing an interesting heresy there, but we are simply incapable of creating a culture.[31]

Sinyavsky's ambivalent attitude toward liberalism and Western democracy shows the split between the philosophical and the practical sides of his personality. In his everyday life as a teacher, critic, and citizen, Sinyavsky worked for liberalization, and in many of his articles he assumed the guise of a defense attorney for writers whose reputations were still on trial. But when he engages in philosophical speculation, in which liberalism cannot serve as a modus operandi, he perceives its groundlessness as an ultimate response to life. For Sinyavsky, liberalism is always a means, never an end, an adjective masquerading as a noun:

I'll never understand what this "freedom of choice" is about which the liberal philosophy carries on so. . . . Freedom is always negative and presupposes an absence, a void striving for the most rapid possible fulfillment.[32]

Sinyavsky regards modern man as twice fallen—once from paradise (by original sin), and once again by his fall from the Christian universe of symbols and sacraments that had connected him to both God and nature and made the year a spiritual journey marked by fasts and holy days. Soviet Man (Homo Soveticus) he views as having fallen yet another time, from the "dark and magical night" of Stalinism into the prosaic, utterly secular, and faceless rule of the bureaucrats.

Though free to travel immense distances and having access to fabulous amounts of information, modern man is in Sinyavsky's view increasingly cut off from himself and from "historical and cosmic life." Sinyavsky's description of peasants, although stylized, even idealized, are perhaps based as much on his trips to the north of Russia as on his reading:

The peasant, before he picked up his spoon—it used to be— would cross himself and with this one reflex gesture unite himself with earth and heaven, with the past and the future.[33]

Whether or not this image of the Russian peasant is valid doesn't very much matter here. What does matter is that Sinyavsky, by taking such a point of view, seems to place himself in the company of those modern religious thinkers who tend to look with nostalgia toward the real or imagined religious unity of the past. Whereas a sceptic would point out that the peasant crosses himself entirely by reflex and would consider the action an empty one, Sinyavsky interprets that reflex as proof of how deeply Christianity had entered men—it had penetrated their nervous systems and become a reflex, a habit. It is highly unlikely that Sinyavsky, on the basis of that nostalgia, would approve a social-political movement with a return to the past as its banner. His nostalgia should rather be seen as a manifestation of his longing for unity. Sinyavsky has kept the essential Christian vision, but he has much too much historical sense to look upon the past with anything but affection and regret.

If there is a link between the peasant crossing himself and the modern world, it would have to be the church, which once before in Russian history, after the Mongol invasion of Kievan Russia, preserved the national identity. In Sinyavsky's opinion the sin of modern Christianity is that it has accommodated itself to the modern world, thereby betraying its own necessarily conservative nature. Here it is somewhat difficult to determine whether he is speaking about the Orthodox Church, which had been under state control long before the Revolution, or about Christianity in general. He points out that the church exists to help men save their souls, maintain a religious vision of life, and struggle against the temptations of the world, despair, and the evidence of the senses:

The church cannot but be conservative as long as it wishes to remain faithful to tradition. It does not have the right to say one thing today, another tomorrow, depending on the interests of progress.[34]

The modern church suffers from an excess of good manners and has forgotten how to administer the tongue-lashings at which the prophets were so adept. The true Christian hero is not the sage, but the man who struggles against evil with the only weapon he has, the readiness to die for what he believes in. Death, which provides the only crack in the secular world-view allowing man a breath and glimpse of the infinite, is now shown to have a direct bearing on the world of human affairs; the man who is not afraid of death, accepts it as part of life and as a sign of man's participation in the mysteries of the cosmos, is at the same time liberated from the fear of the authorities, the powers of the world, whose strength derives from their ability to imprison and execute. Thus the retreat from ethics to solitary contemplation itself gives rise to new ethical possibilities by providing a spiritual foundation for resistance to evil. No doubt it was these moments of celestial clarity that inspired Sinyavsky with the courage to face his trial and his exile and also helped to heal the wound in his divided life, a wound both required and forbidden by his circumstances, and which he inflicted upon himself as with a ritual knife.

The essence of Sinyavsky's stripped-down Christianity is not ethics but metaphysics, the cleaving to God. The only thing of importance is that men keep God alive in their minds and hearts, and with the passion of a prayer Sinyavsky exclaims:

God! Better that I err in Your name than that I forget You. Better that I sin by You than that I forget You. Better that I let my soul perish than that You disappear from sight.[35]

An ethic that does however emerge quite naturally from his religious vision has many of the features common to all religious systems. Aldous Huxley has called this ethic "the perennial philosophy." It has as its first principle the direct relating of one human being to another, the recognition of

an equal humanity in another person, what Martin Buber
termed in a shorthand expression "I and Thou." The comparison of Sinyavsky with Buber is not haphazard; it has
already been made by Mihajlov, who pointed out that their
thought has certain similarities and that one of Sinyavsky's
Fantastic Stories bears the title "Thou and I," though it
refers to schizophrenia and not, as does Buber's *I and Thou*,
to loving thy neighbor. The act of dropping the façade of
the ego, which Sinyavsky refers to as "capital," is itself an
act of liberation at once profoundly human and divine.
Sinyavsky is philosophic but not a philosopher, he is build-
ing no system, inventing no new vocabulary. This puts him
in the mainstream of the Russian tradition, in which literature and philosophy are not as a rule entirely differentiated.
Sinyavsky describes the ethical moment quite simply:

A man becomes truly close and dear when he loses his official
designations—his profession, his name, his age.[36]

Toward the end of *Thought Unaware* he connects that
state of returned innocence (redemption, liberation) with
falling asleep, childhood, and death. Sleep and death dissolves the ego, and the young child has not yet experienced
its imperious demands and illusory separateness. There is
something innocent about the old as well, especially old
women, for they live close to the mystery of death and far
from the grotesque games required by sex.

Sinyavsky sent *Thought Unaware* abroad together with
The Makepeace Experiment, thereby indicating that he
wished them to be viewed as related works, just as he had

previously done with *On Socialist Realism* and *The Trial Begins*. Because of their essential similarity, the two sets of works gives us a clear insight into the creative process as it operates in Sinyavsky. In both cases we have a speculative work accompanied by a novella in which the speculations are personified and dramatized, or at least have a direct genetic relation to the action. In fact, however, in Sinyavsky's works, there are no real boundaries between the speculative and artistic: the musical composition of *Thought Unaware*, the passionate ironies and paradoxes of *On Socialist Realism*, and the ideological dilemmas and the historical parables of the fictional works indicate a single creative process at work, rather than the translation of ideas from one medium to another. Sinyavsky is an artist of the intellect and the imagination thinking his way into the depths of his psyche, where he finds the images around which to build his stories, which are in turn clarified by further intellectual elaboration. The best of his images are spontaneous poetic creations, not illustrations of ideas, but images radiating ideas. And where this is not the case his work suffers accordingly. The inner, subjective side should not be overly stressed, for in the end Sinyavsky always returns to the world. He attempts to bring together the images of daily life and images of "fantastic" spirituality, and the juxtaposition of these images provides the comic element (God and the Electrician, the clairvoyant and the secret policeman in "The Icicle"). To unite is to redeem, and with every work he wrote he came a little closer to uniting the world of Tertz with the world of Sinyavsky.

6

Science and Fiction:
Fantastic Stories

Science occupies a place of pride both in the rather undefined cultural mythology of the West and in the Communist religion of history. Without making a prolonged detour into the past, we can simply state that the trinity of logic, science, and technology has been gradually moving toward a position of preeminence in human thinking and affairs since the Renaissance and that, although its disappearance from the scene is hardly to be predicted, it is no longer regarded as an unmitigated blessing. Quite the reverse, science (including logic and technology) has in recent times come under attack in both the West and in the Soviet Union, for interestingly different reasons. The revolt against science in the West has many causes—the specter of the Bomb, pollution, the wastefulness of capitalist society, the amount of information available to the citizenry which can serve to stimulate awareness, as well as a certain chiliastic ennui. In the Soviet Union, where the state controls industry and information, a different picture emerges. There science has been put into the service of repression (not that it hasn't in various places and at various times in the West). The relationship between science and the state is every bit as important as that between the state and literature, and it is reflected in nearly all the writings of the dissidents, a term which here may be extended to include such prominent scientists as Sakharov and Medvedev. As the Soviet Union in its post-Stalin phase pays greater and greater attention to preserving appearances, the simple but effective brutality of Stalin is being replaced by more subtle means of coercion and repression in which science is playing a leading role. Until now moral neutrality has been seen as the very essence of science (and it is, of the scientific method), and attempts to create a "science" on the basis of ideology (Lysenko) or nationality (the Nazis) have proved murderous and futile. Science is neutral, but politics and politicians are not, and it is an unfortunate but inescapable fact that the distance from the laboratory to the offices of the secret police is a very short one.

It has often been said that Russia has suffered greatly from the lack of a tradition of freedom, but this observation has been too frequently restricted to the area of political and social freedom. The lack of freedom in the nineteenth century created an oppressive atmosphere that fostered, as Sinyavsky notes in *On Socialist Realism*, a craving for belief and a sense of continual urgency, neither of which is conducive to developing a tradition of healthy scepticism. Science grew out of a tradition in which the absolutism of religion was opposed by enlightened scepticism and empiricism. Russia imported science and the worship of it, but the tradition from which science was born travels less easily.

Extravagant hopes were placed in science, and the nine-teenth-century radical Russian intelligentsia looked forward to a paradise of justice and plenty based on science and reason. Science was seen not only as a means of solving social problems when coupled with a social revolution, but also as a tool for solving the riddles of matter and history. But even though in Russia science and technology were less developed than in the West, a rebellion against the scientific method and its assumptions took early and strong root in Russia. Dostoevsky, with his uncanny instinct for finding the menaces concealed in blessings, saw in science a force that would imprison man in a three-dimensional, thoroughly material universe in which the longing for God and the belief in the immortality of the soul would be con-sidered unhealthy anachronisms. His defense of the divine irrationality of man did not develop in a vacuum, but in the context of a revolt against a specific mystique.

The writers of the post-Stalin period have a very differ-ent bone to pick than did Dostoevsky, the Symbolist phi-losophers who were his followers, and Yevgeny Zamiatin, whose antiutopian novel *We* incarnates Dostoevsky's for-mula, two plus two is the beginning of death. What Do-stoevsky foresaw and Zamiatin fictionalized are for the post-Stalin intelligentsia past and current history. The voice decoder whose development plays a central part in the workings of Solzhenitsyn's *The First Circle*, Anatoly Marchenko's protest in *My Testimony* against camp dis-cipline by starvation based on a precise estimate of human caloric needs, and Sinyavsky's paranoid fantasy of a psychoscope that peers into people's minds are all instances of this concern. Other writers like Valery Tarsis (author of *Ward No.* 7, a fictionalized account of a Soviet punitive psychiatric ward) and Zhores Medvedev (whose *A Question of Madness*, describes his own experiences in such a ward) are more concerned with the state's use of the social sciences, particularly psychiatry, as punitive instruments. As is all too evident, the neutrality of science relates to the creation of hypotheses and the conducting of experiments and not to their implementation; if the central philosophical concern of the "dissidents" is the defense of man, then science at this moment in Soviet history can not be seen entirely as an ally. Here one must distinguish among three types of attitudes: intelligent people do not reject, on principle or in practice, the obvious blessings of science—after all, it is one thing to be antirationalist and quite another to refuse anesthesia; one may or may not accept the philosophical implications of science at a given moment—for Darwin and Einstein science led to the mysteries of contemplation whereas for Dostoevsky or Tolstoy it was an agent of man's spiritual destruction; but the incorporation of science into the state and its transformation into an instrument of repression is another matter entirely, and one with which modern Russian writers must deal since it is an integral part of their reality.

Mihajlo Mihajlov, in his book on Sinyavsky, places him in the tradition of the irrationalists who revolt against science on metaphysical grounds, bracketing his name with the names of Dostoevsky, Rozanov, Berdyaev, and Shestov.

In Mihajlov's view the sinister collaboration of science and totalitarian government is by no means an aberration but is inevitable because both systems of thought are by nature tyrannical: "Every science, as an end in itself, is totalitarian and there undoubtedly exists a close tie between social totalitarianism and the spirit of science." [1] Mihajlov sees science as possessed by the same sort of diabolical dialectic that perverted communism by confusing ends and means; science no longer serves man but uses, exploits, and tyrannizes him. He argues that the rebellion against the inhuman rationalism of science and the rebellion against the equally inhuman rationalism of *raison d'état* are one and the same, and this argument must apply with special vigor to the Soviet Union with its "scientific" political philosophy and its use of science in repression. The battle is between the spiritual view of man as divine in origin and with an immortal soul and the materialist view of him as an evanescent accident with no moral nature except that created in him by his society, his class.

In the course of his argument Mihajlov touches on an idea that has rarely been treated in works of literary criticism or intellectual history, namely the relationship between science and the formal aspects of prose fiction. It is an idea he suggests and employs without much elaboration, and its assumptions and implications should be examined since they relate so directly to the work of Sinyavsky. Dostoevsky was a fierce enemy of the scientific image of man, and for him freedom and humanity were synonymous, and one's irrationality, the assertion of one's individuality as a value superior to self-interest, was proof of one's freedom. Yet this philosophy manifests itself in the actions and discussions of his characters, not in the artistic form of his works. Of course Dostoevsky strains at the bonds of realism by compressing time, by introducing extreme forms of behavior and irrational material (dreams, hallucinations) into his novels, and even by employing sentence structures that, with all their breaks and interruptions, suggest the percolating of the unconscious, but he never breaks these bonds. Nor has Solzhenitsyn truly smashed the scientific image of man, according to Mihajlov, who contends that the essentially realistic mode of narrative which Solzhenitsyn uses is close to the scientific vision of man because it is based primarily on sense data. In Mihajlov's terms the "test tube" stands for this realistic mode, the three-dimensional material, primarily visual presentation of the world:

> Russian literature today has two poles, which, however far apart they lie, nevertheless meet. One pole is Tertz, the man who breaks through the test tube. The other is Solzhenitsyn, for whom the test tube is the greatest reality. But because Solzhenitsyn describes the test tube so truthfully, he prepares its destruction. The relationship between Solzhenitsyn and Tertz exactly parallels that between Tolstoy and Dostoevsky.[2]

But Dostoevsky did not smash the "test tube": his works, with one interesting and very relevant exception, "The Dream of a Ridiculous Man" (Son smeshnogo cheloveka," 1877), belong to a special type of double realism, close to Symbolism, where higher and lower realities are coordinated. This story's subtitle, "A Fantastic Story" ("fantas-ticheskiy rasskaz"), is undoubtedly the source of Sinyav-sky's title for his short stories, just as Dostoevsky's concept of "higher realism" (*vysshiy realizm*) can be felt in the call for a new art with which Sinyavsky's *On Socialist Realism* closes.

"The Dream of a Ridiculous Man" has many elements in common with Sinyavsky's tales: an exaltation of the sub-jective and irrational as the source and measure of reality, a sense that sin is inevitable, that every human being repeats the Fall, and that the effects of the scientific world view are dangerous: "But we have science and with its aid we will find the truth again, and this time we will accept it consciously. Knowledge is higher than feeling, the con-sciousness of life is higher than life." [3] This story, one of his most beautiful and moving short works, contains the whole of Dostoevsky's philosophy in its quintessential form. Sinyavsky, writing some eighty years later and with the experience of literary modernism behind him, was not afraid to take Dostoevsky's hint and develop it fully, to move away from the form-content relationship of realism and enter into an investigation of the psyche itself. In Sinyavsky's six fantastic stories it is consciousness itself that is both the subject and the medium; the objective world of people and things recedes into the background or suddenly looms in the foreground but is always seen from a point of view whose indidivuality is emphasized by its abnormality. In a curious way, these stories are slices of life, not a slice of the beef and blood of life, but tissue-thin

specimens of consciousness, stained so that the peculiar and
the aberrant stand out. Each of these stories is concerned
with a specific type of consciousness shaped by a definite
psychological force. Though all these stories stress the
more exotic and fantastic aspects of the human psyche, the
realities of Soviet life are never lost sight of; in fact, Sinyavsky uses these extreme states of mind, themselves products
of the strains and pressures of Soviet society, to reveal sides
of Soviet life to which realism is blind. It is the interplay of
the social and the subjective that fascinates Sinyavsky, and
as a result these tales are at once satirical and philosophic.

Two of the six stories are entirely successful ("Pkhentz,"
undated, and "The Icicle," 1961), while two others ("At
the Circus" and "You and I") share some of the structural
weaknesses of *The Trial Begins* and are, in fact, the earliest
stories, having been written in 1955 and 1959 respectively.
"The Tenants" (1959) and "Graphomaniacs" (1960) represent a transitional stage in which Sinyavsky is clarifying
and simplifying his narrative technique. All these stories
seek to disorient the reader by dislocating his sense of
reality. The stories that achieve this effect most completely
are first-person narratives in which the reader identifies
with the narrator, and the least successful stories employ
the excessive Pirandellian toying with the narrative that
hinders the narrative in *The Trial Begins*.

"At the Circus," the earliest of Sinyavsky's known
writings and one of the best of the fantastic stories, switches
back and forth from a first to a third person narrator much
more gracefully than does "You and I." The plot, as in all

these stories, is minimal, the tale is in the telling. A young man, Konstantin Petrovich, is charmed by the Manipulator at a circus; transformed into a pickpocket, Konstantin becomes rich, lives high on the hog and then, going against his better instincts, agrees to pull a housebreaking job. The house, supposedly empty, is, in fact, inhabited by the Manipulator, who wakes up and refuses to be intimidated by Konstantin's gun. Konstantin shoots him and is sentenced to twenty years for murder. Trying to escape, he too is shot and killed.

The influence of two Russian masters is obvious in this tale: The Babel of *The Tales of Odessa*, exuberant, romantic stories of colorful gangsters, crossed with the dark comedy of Nikolai Gogol. The theme of temptation by the devil (or a devil-like figure, the Manipulator) is central to many of Gogol's stories ("The Portrait," "Nevsky Prospect") and to his novel *Dead Souls*. The description of the Manipulator—shiny, foreign, repulsive—corresponds almost exactly to Gogol's own image of the devil:

But all were outshone by a performer called the Manipulator, a sort of genteel little intellectual of foreign appearance. He had jet-black hair with a part as smooth as if he'd had the bare patch cut out by an electric razor run along a ruler. Below it he had a moustache and the complete outfit—a natty little tie, patent-leather shoes.[4]

His actions and manner, besides being devilish, are replete with Gogolesque nasal humor—the Manipulator puts a wine glass under someone's nose, squeezes the nose, and out comes golden soda water, which a young lady drinks down with a polite "merci." The connection of art with the criminal and demonic is strongly suggested and Faustian motifs are also present. But it would be unwise to treat this tale as merely an allegory of art, for Sinyavsky has more ambitious designs here. In fact, he is creating a parable about the Russian national character much as Leskov did in *The Enchanted Wanderer* (*Ocharovanny Strannik*) and "The Left-handed Smith" ("Levsha"). The luster and technology of the West hold the Russian hero Konstantin spellbound, and although they lead him to his doom, they do so with the full cooperation of his extravagant nature, which throws caution to the winds and longs for mighty, irrational experiences (sex and vodka, or, to use Sinyavsky's synonyms, black magic and white magic). The fable-like quality of this story is underscored by the use of one of the typical devices of the Russian folk tale (*skazka*): the magnitude of Konstantin's sexual exploits with his girlfriend Tamara can only be indicated by their ineffability: "Konstantin bathed on a bachelor basis with a girl called Tamara, and they got up to such acrobatics in these cubicles as can neither be fabled in story, nor portrayed by pen." [5] Sinyavsky displayed the same satirical, intimate affection toward Konstantin in this story that he does toward Russians in general in the aphorisms of *Thought Unaware* and in his novel *The Makepeace Experiment*. Pushkin wrote a poem about Chaadaev, the first to accuse Russia of lacking a history, in which he said that in Athens, Chaadaev would have been a Pericles, whereas in Russia the best he could hope for was the rank of officer in the cavalry. Those sentiments are echoed here when the old Jew, Solomon Moiseyevich, says to Konstantin: "Now, in England, Konstantin Petrovich, you'd be an inventor . . . or a member of Parliament . . . a minister without portfolio." [6] There is also a Chaadaevian vision of the Russians and history, but pronounced with affection and not scorn, of the Russian need to astonish the West instead of producing a stable and viable culture:

The heart beats about in your breast like a bird in a cage; your soul is rent in fragments by love and pity, while you keep pouring out more and more vodka to continue the torment, until finally you rise to your full height from the befouled parquet floor and bark out a series of unprintable obscenities so that all Europe can hear you.[7]

In a single sentence, all the attributes of the Russian national character (or clichés about it)—prodigious, "mystical" drinking, devil-may-care recklessness, metaphysical complications, the need to suffer—are present, treated half in earnest, half in jest, in typical Sinyavsky fashion.

Konstantin's foil is Solomon, a wise but alcoholic Jew, who is close to the Russians and yet not able to penetrate the mystery of their character:

Everyone knew that three years before, Solomon's wife, a lascivious Russian bitch, had run away, after first robbing him then disgracing him with the hairdresser Gennady, aged sixteen. He knew women and feared them, having every reason to do so. But what could he understand about the Russian national character, this Solomon Moiseyevich? [8]

In this story Sinyavsky is playing with not only the characteristics traditionally ascribed to the Russian personality but the special relationship between Russian and Jew. This relationship may be seen as a subtheme of Sinyavsky's fiction, appearing as the historical background for *The Trial Begins* and playing a key role in the plot of *The Makepeace Experiment*. It cannot be said that Sinyavsky is pushing any particular point of view, but he is exploring a subject that has been largely neglected in Russian literature. If we look at the portraits of Jews in Russian literature of the nineteenth century we find little of human or artistic interest. To some degree this was a result of the officially ghettoized life of most Russian Jews in this period, and the Russian intelligentsia, as it became more progressive, put its energies into establishing contact with the broad masses of the peasantry rather than with the Jews. Whatever the causes, in nineteenth-century Russian literature Jews were mostly the butt of satire and caricature, Gogol's Yankel and Dostoevsky's Jew in *Notes from the House of the Dead* being but two examples. It should be pointed out that Jews receive a very different treatment in nineteenth-century Polish literature; the novel *Meir Ezofowicz* (1878), by one of the greatest Polish novelists, Eliza Orzeszkowa, is a detailed and realistic account of Jewish life, and the Polish national epic, *Pan Tadeusz* (1834) by Adam Mickiewicz, has its Jewish innkeeper Jankiel, who is shown in a sympathetic, even heroic light.[9] But the Revolution broke down all existing patterns of Russian society, and many of the early Bolshevik leaders, for example, were Jews. Jews began to be treated seriously in Soviet literature, both by Jewish authors like Babel and non-Jewish ones like Fadeev.

Because of the restrictions that were soon imposed on Soviet literature, the Jewish-Russian relationship was never probed in depth; only Vasily Rozanov, who wrote both pro- and anti-Semitic works had managed to take the lid off the subject. Although Rozanov may have been speaking for himself alone, it is more likely that his reactions to the pogroms of the Black Hundreds and the Beyliss trial were representative of those of a certain layer of the Russian petit bourgeoisie, with this difference: Rozanov's lack of moral standards allowed him to speak his mind without shame, whereas others who thought as he did confided their thoughts only to intimates out of hypocrisy. The position of the Jews in Russia can be likened, *mutatis mutandis*, to that of the Negroes in the United States in that both have been considered aliens who exist in the midst of a culture to which they stand as a living reproach. Both have served (and continue to serve) as a focus for unconscious emotions, targets for projections of sexual energy and hostility (lynchings, pogroms), and the relationship of Jew and Russian, like that of black and white Americans, is still murky, volatile, and dangerous.

"You and I" is a mixed success, in part because it deals with both paranoia and schizophrenia. The story would have worked better had Sinyavsky limited himself to paranoia, a disorder that is widespread and hard to distinguish from common sense in societies which offer it so much genuine fuel. This is one of the recurrent concerns of Nadezhda Mandelstam in her memoirs, *Hope against Hope:*

An existence like this leaves its mark. We all become slightly unbalanced mentally—not exactly ill, but not normal either: suspicious, mendacious, confused and inhibited in our speech. . . . Every section of the population has been through the terrible sickness caused by terror, and none has so far recovered, or become fit again for civic life. It is an illness that is passed on to the next generation, so that the sons pay for the sins of the fathers and perhaps only the grandchildren begin to get over it—or at least it takes on a different form with them.[10]

The opening lines of "You and I" seem to draw the reader into the story by addressing him directly, but later developments show the "you" involved here is really one half of the narrator's personality conversing with the other:

From the very first, this affair had a strange flavor. On the pretext of celebrating his silver wedding anniversary, Genrikh Ivanovich Graube invited four colleagues, including you, to his apartment, and he pressed you so hard to come that evening that it seemed as though your presence was the main object of the get-together.[11]

The scene at the anniversary party catches the nature of paranoia, extreme subjectivity plus terror, perfectly. The narrator thinks that the women present, with one exception, are all in fact NKVD agents who have gone so far in their disguise as to wear lace underwear in case he gets fresh, that the other guests are signaling each other with the clatter of their silverware, and that a huge eye first watches them and then slowly recedes into the wallpaper. Since no point of view except the narrator's is given as a source of perception and a standard of reality, the reader himself experiences paranoia. The party scene is a further development of the bureaucrats' banquet in *The Trial Begins*, but now it is the narrator's hallucinations instead of his remarks that reveal the dangers hidden in placid bureaucrats. Sinyavsky is at his best in his description of ordinary events becoming charged with sinister significance by the narrator's obsessions: Graube, afraid that a politically indiscreet remark he has made may be used against him, offers to go down on his knees as a sign of repentance and submission:

> But you were not to be taken in. You were quick to see the higher strategy that lay behind this humiliating posture. One's defenses are more easily penetrated from below. A man on his knees can grab you by the legs and throw you on your back.[12]

Like many of Sinyavsky's other stories, "You and I" deliberately echoes the classics of Russian literature. The influence of Gogol's "Notes of a Madman," which portrays a mind gradually crumbling into madness, can be felt here, and the theme of the flight from women, the subject of Gogol's play *The Marriage*, is one more instance of Sinyavsky's conscious extension of Russian literary traditions. A Gogolesque predilection for rapturous descriptions of food and grotesque or vulgarly lyrical depictions of women becomes merged into a single metaphor: "Her raised elbow looked like a duck's wing that had been picked clean." [13] The theme of schizophrenia, as opposed to paranoia, works poorly, draws too much from literature (Dostoevsky's *The Double*), and remains a trick of the narrative. Hints of Olesha are to be found in whimsical descriptive details, for example, the comparison of a snowstorm and a parachute attack on a sleeping city. As in several other fantastic stories, Sinyavsky kills off his hero, a too-easy solution, one that he avoids in the more sophisticated tales in this series.

In "Tenants" as in all the other fantastic stories, three elements are blended—experiments in form, philosophic problems, and satire on Soviet life. More precisely, his desire to depict consciousness itself leads Sinyavsky to experiment with narrative techniques, and the grotesque perceptions which result present the Soviet world in a satirical light. This story consists entirely of a one-sided conversation of the narrator in which the replies of the other person, a drunkard and writer, are never reported but only hinted at by the ongoing monologue, a device also used by the Polish satirist Sławomir Mrożek in his short story "Confession." Since the narrator claims to be a creature from the realm of elves and witches, and since no other point of view is present, we have no way of knowing whether he is telling the fictional truth, or whether he is quite mad, or whether the entire thing is the drunken fantasy of the silent writer. Thus the narrative in a straightforward way presents the reader with three possible orientations, with the result that he has none. On the social level the story is a satire on Soviet housing and the hellish problem that arise from sharing bathrooms and kitchens, but instead of treating the subject with realistic comedy in the manner of Zoshchenko, he metaphorizes the situation by turning it into a literal pandemonium. At the same time Sinyavsky is suggesting something of the fantastic side of human nature, for it turns out that the tenants are not human beings but elemental creatures driven from nature by industrialization:

And soon only water nymphs were left. And even they—well, you know, yourself—the industrialization of natural resources. Make way for technology! Streams, rivers, and lakes began to smell of chemical substances. Methylhydrate, toluene. Fishes simply died and floated belly upward. As for the water nymphs, they'd pop out and somehow cough up all that river water, and there'd be tears (believe it or not) of grief and despair in their eyes. Seen it myself. The whole of their voluptuous bosoms covered with ringworm, eczema, and (if you'll forgive my saying so) signs of recurrent venereal disease. . . . Incidentally, there's a former water nymph living in our apartment, as freely and easily as could be. According to her identity card she's a Sofya Frantsevna Vinter. . . . Runs around in a fustian robe and does aquatic exercises from morning till evening.[14]

The theme of the official identity forced on one by society versus one's own secret and fantastic nature will find its fullest expression in the story "Pkhentz" and, in national rather than personal terms, in the novel *The Makepeace Experiment*. In *Thought Unaware* we saw Sinyavsky pining for preindustrial, rural Russia, where peasants connected themselves to the cosmic and historical by the reflex of crossing themselves. Here, in this story, he is wondering what has happened to the marvelous world of pagan Russian mythology, in other words, he is speaking of the exile of the imagination from the modern world with its "methylhydrate" and "toluene," words that clash so harshly with *rusalka* (water nymph) and the simple words invented by men to name everything in nature. And Sinyavsky comes up with the answer: all those creatures of the imagination have gone into hiding, driven out from the world by science and technology; they have gone back to where they came from and where they cannot be found—in human beings. Jung said much the same thing:

Since the stars have fallen from heaven, and our highest symbols have paled, a secret life holds sway in the unconscious. It is for this reason that we have a psychology today, and for this reason that we speak of the unconscious. All this discussion would be superfluous in an age or culture that possessed symbols. . . . Heaven has become empty space to us, a fair memory of things that once were. But our heart glows, and secret unrest gnaws at the roots of our being.[15]

"Graphomaniacs" is the most successfully comic of the fantastic stories. Since it is a story of, by, and about a Russian writer, it abounds with references, both explicit and implicit, to Russian literature and to all the customs and traditions of its makers. In the making of this tale Sinyavsky the student of literature, and Tertz, the author of daring fictions, worked in close harmony. The story's structure is replete with all the mirror tricks of which Sinyavsky is so fond, for here he is writing about a Russian writer who writes about other Russian writers and who, at the end of the story, sits down to write some Russian literature himself, choosing a title that just happens to be the same title Sinyavsky has chosen. In this case the complexity works with the subject and theme, suggesting the mercurial and harried mind of the writer and also inviting the reader into the creative process by folding time back on itself so that it is shaped like a Möbius strip. (This strip is a favorite visual motif of the Dutch graphic artist Maurits Escher, who, like Sinyavsky, portrays the fantastic world of subjectivity and relativity. Clearly, artists may be completely contemporary in spirit without being in the center of things or having access to the latest, a fact that is obvious and has been forgotten.)

Literature—acts of the imagination, the search for a higher self, speaking the truth to society—is of great importance to Sinyavsky. All of his critical writings stress the seriousness of literature and its responsibilities, and the place of special prominence that he accords the poet recalls the Symbolists' vision of the poet as someone in touch with a higher order. But, unlike the Symbolists, Sinyavsky never loses touch with everyday reality and its grotesque, comic, vulgar, brutal, ultimately endearing details. At every step he fiecrely rejects artificial separations—of mystic intuitions and daily life, of life and art, of satire and philosophy. Sinyavsky does not treat literature as any holy of holies, being well aware how corrupt a business it can be, whether the corruption stems from the monstrous egotism of the writers themselves or from those who would use literature for their own purposes. In "Graphomaniacs," he makes his writers second-rate because they stand for humanity, and also because the writerly nature of writers without talent is not obscured by the dazzle of genius. Besides, talent itself is suspect in Sinyavsky's eyes, for it leads to an exaggerated sense of self-importance. Writing's obsessive side is best satirized in the irate words of a writer's discontented wife who, by mentioning "butter," for a moment turns the satire back upon herself:

"It would be better if you were an alcoholic. Drug addicts are better. At least they do have lucid intervals. They love their wives and show fondness for their children. Not a scrap of attention do we get. Has time only for the arts. Butter. Four months without work." [16]

Reality does not belong to the experts. Nor do first-rate writers have a monopoly on truth. Ordinary men have moments of great understanding, and writers without talent may have them as well. It is because both ordinary men and talentless writers are powerless to tell what they know that the latter are such a fresh and true symbol of the former. The question of talent or no talent may not even be so important after all; Osip Mandelstam always insisted that he knew he was essentially no different from anyone else and that such knowledge was vital for a Soviet poet. Thus the bliss of creative work is described by Galkin, a genius bereft of talent:

People talk about "making one's mark," "expressing one's personality." But in my opinion every writer is occupied by one thing alone: self-suppression. That's why we labor in the sweat of our brow and cover wagon loads of paper with writing—in the hope of stepping aside, overcoming ourselves, and granting access to thoughts from the air. They arise spontaneously, independently of ourselves. All we do is work and work, and to go farther and farther along the road, mastering ourselves from time to time and giving way to them. Then suddenly— after all, it always is a sudden immediate process—it becomes clear that you composed one thing yourself, so that it's worth-less, while another thing is not yours and you don't dare, don't have the right to do anything with it, either to change it or to improve it. It's not your property! And you retreat in bewil-derment. You're flabbergasted. Not at any particular beauty of the achievement. Simply from terror at your own non-participation in what has taken place.[17]

The thoughts which this passage presents may also be found in aphoristic form in Sinyavsky's musings on the human personality, the ego (which he calls "Capital") in *Thought Unaware*.

The story itself concerns and is narrated by Pavel Ivano-vich Straustin. Using a traditional comic device of Russian fiction, Sinyavsky gives his characters names with a humor-ous significance; Each name is, in one way or another, con-nected with the world of birds—Straustin (Ostrich), Gal-kin (Jackdaw), Grebin (comb). They all behave like males of the species, strutting and displaying their verbal plumage, fighting for a place in the pecking order. Straustin gives us a glimpse of the demimonde of Russian literature, the bottom of the pile, as well as a barrage of remarks on past authors and numerous reflections on the creative process. The incidents around which this tale is constructed are simple: a chance meeting with Galkin, a spat with his wife, a visit to an editorial office, a literary evening. Straustin has all the characteristic flaws of writers, successful or un-successful—he is touchy, full of vainglory and *amour-propre*, vengeful, slightly paranoid, boundlessly ambitious, conceited, and self-pitying. His paranoia reaches its peak when he "discovers" that many great Russian and European writers have stolen lines, even whole paragraphs from him, a reference to Goncharov's delusion that Turgenev was stealing material from him and sending it to Flaubert and other French writers. Russian literature is often commented upon or parodied. Sinyavsky lifts the famous scene in Gogol's *The Inspector General* in which an important note and a hotel bill get mixed up, but in his version it becomes a babel of writers declaiming their own works that gets jumbled; in this scene Sinyavsky acknowledges his debt to Gogol by inserting the line from *Dead Souls:* "O, Rus'! Kuda neseshsia ty?" ("O, Rus, whither doest thou race?"). Straustin loathes those benign and inaccessible establishment editors who continually advise him to study the classics, and he vents his spleen on Chekhov in a passage which, although it seemed a sacrilege to those who presided at Sinyavsky's trial, is simply a means of characterizing Straustin and a jibe at Russian literary necrophilia, with its Egyptian mania for preserving memorabilia:

The classical writers—it's them I hate the most! Before I was so much as born they stole the vacant places. . . . "Read Chekhov, read Chekhov!" people kept on at me all my life, tactlessly suggesting that Chekhov wrote better than I. . . . And how could one fight against them when at Yasnaya Poly-ana even the the fingernails of Leo Tolstoy, cut a thousand years ago and collected by the farsighted Count in a special little bag, are preserved in a special little bag like a holy relic? And it's said that in Yalta, Chekhov's dried-up spit has been collected in special little packets—yes, the actual spit of Anton Pavlovich Chekhov, who is said to have suffered a great deal from the spitting of blood and even died of tuberculosis, which is of course a great exaggeration.

. . . That Chekhov ought to have been taken by his wretched tubercular beard and have his nose shoved in his consumptive hawking that have unfortunately now dried up.[18]

But this tale, as well as being a picture of second-rate literary men, is a smiling allegory of humanity, which is composed of failed geniuses who have much too high an opinion of themselves and yet are treated worse than they deserve.

The last two fantastic stories, "The Icicle" and "Pkhentz," merit special attention because they clearly mark a new stage in the evolution of Sinyavsky-Tertz, a breakthrough into religious consciousness. This breakthrough is accompanied by dramatic improvement in Sinyavsky's technical skills as an artist and by greater daring in his selection of metaphors for the human condition. Whereas the four other fantastic tales deal with states of mind in which the neurotic and the sublime are mixed, muddying each other somewhat, in the last two tales the metaphoric consciousness is no longer tied to identifiable psychological traits, for Sinyavsky's concerns now are the occult and the extraterrestrial. Now the satire proceeds from a very different intuition, not the identification of comic discrepancies, but a vision of man against the background of eternity. Thus the comic becomes brighter, warmer, more loving, and the tragic notes are darker and more ominous. The effect is that of a sudden and radical change in lighting—nothing is added or removed but everything seems new and different. A spiritual leap made it necessary and possible for Sinyavsky to employ bolder devices to express his new sense of life. He took genres (science fiction and the occult) traditionally considered outside the pale of "respectable" literature and breathed full artistic life into them, just as Dostoevsky in *Crime and Punishment* had taken the detective story and made a drama of sin and redemption out of it.

Sinyavsky sent his work abroad in three separate batches —*The Trial Begins* and *On Socialist Realism* in late 1956, *Fantastic Stories* in 1961, and *The Makepeace Experiment* and *Thought Unaware* in 1963: the final page of *On Socialist Realism*, in which he hypothesizes a new art, and "Pkhentz" were sent separately. By dispatching them in this fashion Sinyavsky seemed to indicate that the works sent together should be understood as the result of a common effort and be so treated, and a careful reading of them bears out this supposition. *Fantastic Stories* is the bridge between the early Sinyavsky, who was wrestling with social and historical problems, and the later Sinyavsky whose struggles had been rewarded with a vision of the unity of all things. The story "The Icicle" portrays the step into the religious dimension, and "Pkhentz" treats the tragic loneliness of those with higher knowledge, memories of "other worlds."

As in all the other fantastic stories, the plot line of "The Icicle" is quite simple, though it weaves back and forth in time. Having acquired occult powers (the ability to tell the future and to read people's past and future incarnations), Vasily realizes that Natasha, the woman he loves, will be killed on a certain day by a falling icicle, and he flees with her in an attempt to prevent the inevitable. He is taken into custody by the police, who want to harness his abilities, to use them as headlights on the juggernaut of History. Natasha, no longer protected by Vasily, is killed in the exact place and manner he predicted, and soon after this Vasily loses his powers.

The satire in this tale derives from the contrast of the all-too-human and the supernatural, of man's potential and his actual life. The mixing of the high and the low, the sublime and vulgar, is an old device, but here it is used for not only comic effect but also philosophic purposes. It provides a comic vision of the Fall, of human estrangement from a higher order. The hero himself, the people around him, and especially the police, are all unable to appreciate the source, the nature, and the beauty of the gift. Demonstrating his newly acquired powers at a party, Vasily amazes those present by successfully predicting that a bedbug will crawl out from behind an engraving, a Giorgione he thinks. Even his highest musing on the oneness of life are satirically qualified by his Soviet habits of mind for, apart from his gift, Vasily is a very average Soviet man: "I was also intrigued, from the scientific point of view, by the absence of any connecting links between death and birth." [19] The police's attempts to use Vasily's powers are necessarily comic: they want him to speed up the inevitable progress toward Communism, to give Australia a little nudge in the right direction, but Vasily's gift is cosmic and personal, not historical, and the services he is able to render his country are comically minuscule:

I deciphered a few mysterious telegrams sent by a certain foreign correspondent to a government-inspired newspaper

abroad. I also foretold the fall of the cabinet, forty-eight hours
before it happened, in a certain insignificant country and thus
enabled our diplomats to make their financial overtures in good
time.[20]

The most important philosophical passage in "The Icicle"
concern death, reincarnation, and human nature. What is
most remarkable about them is their emotional tone, in
which the lyrical, the satirical, and hints of the tragic merge
into each other, forming a completely unique tone, the tone
of Sinyavsky's voice and vision. His basic view of life finds
its fullest expression in such passages because the sublime
point of view only makes the quotidian world look more
comic, more tragic. The connectedness and unity of all
phenomena, and the universality of every man are shown
as something essentially funny:

My pigmy self had egotistically resisted the interlopers which,
without warning, had settled in my head, like lice, threatening
a total breakdown of my central nervous system. But now that
I was face to face with nature and its manifest order and neat-
ness, the presence of these other beings gave me nothing but
consolation and pleasure, and made me aware of my depth,
strength, and inner worth. . . . We shall settle inside some
roomy citizen of the future and I think he will not be indifferent to us. . . .
Hey! You there, man of the future! Listen to what I say!
Don't forget to remember me on that quiet summer evening.
Look, I'm smiling at you, I'm smiling in you, I'm smiling
through you. How can I be dead if I breathe in every quiver
of your hand?
Here I am! You thing I don't exist? You think I've dis-
appeared forever? Wait! The dead are singing in your body;
dead souls are droning in your nerves.[21]

Vasily is able to see not only the unity of the world but its immortality as well. There is no death, life is forever alive. Perhaps Sinyavsky's conversation with Pasternak and intimate knowledge of his poetry provided some of the seeds of this very Pasternakian vision; however, unlike Pasternak, Sinyavsky never loses touch with daily realities where terrible (if sometimes comic) pressures are brought to bear on those with higher knowledge, special gifts. This theme is continued in "Pkhentz," which stresses utter loneliness instead of personal tragedy.

Zamoyska is right that Sinyavsky's study of Picasso is "the key to the experiments in style in "The Icicle." It is, in many respects, a cubist tale, except that the Cubists broke up and reorganized space, whereas, of course, Sinyavsky does the same with time. Past, present, and future are superimposed, a collage of tenses. But this story is also a full incarnation of the new art announced at the closure of *On Socialist Realism* for in it Sinyavsky looks with new eyes on the world and man.

"The Icicle" may also be seen as a condensed version of the development of Sinyavsky-Tertz, the slow process of self-discovery telescoped into a single breakthrough. The words spoken by Vasily about his notes can be applied to their author:

I write this story as a castaway tells of his distress. Sitting on a piece of wreckage, or stranded on a desert island, he throws a bottle with a letter into the stormy sea, in the hope that the waves and the wind will carry it to people who will read it and learn the truth long after its poor author is dead.

But the question is: Will the bottle ever reach its destination? Will a sailor haul it up by the neck with his strong hand and will he shed tears of pity on the deck of his ship? Or will the seal gradually be corroded by brine, the paper eaten away, and the unknown bottle, filled with bitter sea water, dash against a reef and come to rest, motionless, on the bottom of the ocean? [22]

I am convinced that most books are letters to the future.[23]

If the stress in "The Icicle" is on inward discovery, in "Pkhentz" it falls rather on the isolation and sadness of the outsider. The metaphor is now one of space, not time, not of a man acquiring contact with another world, but of a creature from another world anxious lest, among men, he forgets his lost homeland. In both stories the same elements are intermingled—satire, philosophy, innovation, and spirirual autobiography—but here the tone is more somber, the satire more painful, for the story is really a portrait of man after the Fall, the Expulsion.

It would be a mistake to consider this story merely an allegory of alienation in the social sense of the word. Sinyavsky is much too shrewd to accept the cliché of the gifted individual versus a brutal, philistine society, both because he knows that artistically that pattern has been worn thin and because that sort of egocentric Romanticism is foreign to him. But Sinyavsky is a Romantic in his own fashion, and "Pkhentz" has connections with the earliest Romantic stances, which saw alienation primarily as a metaphysical condition. Man is ill at ease in the world; he does not feel at home there because his nature is spiritual, belongs to another dimension of existence, and thus he feels his life to be an exile, an Expulsion, a Fall. In this connection it is enough to remember Wordsworth's new-born soul "trailing clouds of glory," or Lermontov's poem "The Angel," in which the birth of a human being is depicted as a descent from a higher to a lower level of being.

"Pkhentz" has little plot; rather, it has the movement of a slow and puzzling epiphany, for the reader is only gradually made aware that the narrator (and hero) is an alien from another world, one so far away that, when he stares at the stars at night, he doesn't even know in which direction to be homesick. The title itself has no meaning (except in the language of the narrator's planet, a language which he can hardly remember), and instead of orienting the reader, it throws him off balance, thereby readying him for the unearthly perceptions of the narrator. These perceptions are comic and grotesque because they are formed in a mind whose standards of beauty are not human. When Tolstoy devastated the artificiality of the opera in *War and Peace* by refusing to accept the conventions of perception and calling scenery painted cardboard instead of trees and houses, he did so to shock the reader into innocence of perception by making the familiar strange again (*ostranenie*); Sinyavsky accomplishes the same, but instead of focusing on the artificial, his alien's eyes estrange the most normal aspects of human life. This is food:

Food stood on the table, steaming and evil smelling. The sadism of cookery has always amazed me. Would-be chickens are eaten in liquid form. The innards of pigs are stuffed with their own flesh. A gut that's swallowed itself garnished with stillborn chickens. That, in fact, is what scrambled egg with sausage is.[24]

This is a woman's body:

It was—I repeat—horrible. I found that her whole body was of the same unnatural whiteness as her neck, face, and hands. A pair of white breasts dangled in front. At first I took them for secondary arms, amputated above the elbow. But each of of them terminated in a round nipple like a bell-push.

Farther on, and right down to her legs, the whole available space was occupied by a spherical belly. That is where the food swallowed in the course of the day collects in a heap. Its lower half was overgrown with curly hair like a little head. . . .

I caught a glimpse of something resembling a human face. Only it didn't look female to me, but more like an old man's face, unshaven and baring its teeth.[25]

The narrator appears at first to be a hunchback, but his hunch is in fact an extra set of arms covered with eyes, as are his feet; he exists on water and has no greater pleasures than to free his seeing feet from shoes, which have already caused one eye to go blind, and to admire his beauty from a dozen angles at once, in true cubist fashion. But in the Soviet Union, where his space ship had crashed killing everyone but him, the state defines his identity:

Why have I spent thirty years pretending to be somebody else, like a criminal? Andrei Kazimirovich Sushinsky. Half-Polish, half-Russian. Aged 61. Disabled. Not a Party-member. Bachelor. No relatives, no children. Never been abroad.[26]

The dilemma of the official and the private identity was, of course, one Sinyavsky knew well, and he and his hero have several points of similarity—the first name, the Polish background (Sinyavsky has Polish blood on his father's side), the ironic "never been abroad"; and the word "pkhentz," which the hero remembers from his native tongue, sounds suspiciously like "Tertz."

"Pkhentz" contains a disgust with humanity that reminds one of Jonathan Swift and the Tolstoy of *Resurrection*. Nothing is spared—language, the human body, human institutions, culture—all appear hideous when seen from the perspective of ultimate alienation and despair. But this is not, one feels, the dead-end despair of modern Western literature, but a stage in a pilgrimage which Solzhenitsyn, in the prose-poem "A Prayer" ("Molitva"), has described as "that amazing path through despair that led me here, from where even I could send humanity some reflection of Your radiance."

History versus the People

I've even been called a Slavophile.

Andrei Sinyavsky,
at his trial

The Makepeace Experiment (*Lyubimov*) was written, according to Sinyavsky's testimony at his trial, during the years 1961–1962, although it was not published in the West until 1965. Along with *On Socialist Realism* and *The Trial Begins* it was part of the specific literary evidence used by the prosecution against him, and thus Sinyavsky was tried on the basis of his first works and his last. In the fact that the works which define the beginning and the end of his literary career as Abram Tertz are the ones by which he was tried, there is a grotesque poetic justice and a sharp irony as well. With his first two works Sinyavsky opened himself up to the confusion, the contradiction, and the despair that are all inevitable results of moving from one level of understanding to another, but *The Makepeace Experiment* is a literary achievement marked by great contemplative serenity, forgiving humor, and loving acceptance of the Russian people and their history. The titles of his first and last novels convey their differences in tone—*On Trial*, with all the jagged emotion suggested by that phrase, and

Lyubimov, from the Russian word *lyubit,* "to love." Sinyavsky himself pointed this out at his trial when his novel was compared with Saltykov-Shchedrin's acrid satire, *The History of a Town (Istoriya odnogo goroda,* 1869–1870), which, like *The Makepeace Experiment,* localizes its action and implications in a small, provincial Russian town, in Shchedrin's case called Glupov, from the Russian word *glupy,* meaning "stupid" or "foolish."

Sinyavsky was fortunate to have been able to finish writing *The Makepeace Experiment* before he was arrested, for the serenity it radiates indicates that he had achieved the reconstruction of his values that he had set out in 1956 to accomplish. A temporal and spiritual equilibrium is at work here, and if the years 1950–1956 were a time of crisis for Sinyavsky, then the creative years 1956–1962 were a time of conscious search, healing, and self-discovery.

In *Fantastic Stories,* Sinyavsky was primarily concerned with the whorls and loops of subjectivity, the uniqueness of individual consciousness and the loneliness of individual fate, but in *The Makepeace Experiment* he returns to the collective, the people as hero, whose primary feat (*podvig*) is their survival of "history." A further irony obtains here: in *The Makepeace Experiment,* Sinyavsky has written a true tale of the collective (albeit a fairy tale), something few orthodox Soviet writers have managed, but of course, from the government's point of view, the implications of the work point in exactly the wrong direction. Sinyavsky's position now resembles Tolstoy's in *War and Peace* except that, instead of combating the myth of the hero, Sinyavsky takes on the myth of the leader, the ruler, and also the communist myth of the people as the bearers of historical change. This confrontation of myth and reality (or counter myth) is necessarily comic, as is any deflating of pretense, for in Sinyavsky's view "history" is not the people's mission but their enemy; they are drawn into its storms and, by not resisting, survive. There is, as Sinyavsky hinted, much that can be called Slavophile in this novel, though with certain very definite qualifications. Sinyavsky's attitude toward his people is hardly one of unadulterated reverence or messianic expectation but rather one of affectionate and humorous intimacy, as in a family which has its own customs, jokes, and legends, but whose members all know each other too well ever to take themselves entirely seriously. The Slavophilism of the nineteenth century had a definite programmatic approach to the social problems of the day and in fact arose in response to these problems, reflecting one effort at their solution. But Sinyavsky is writing after the "solution," and his position is explorative, not programmatic; he seeks the balance between historical change and constancy, between what passes and what abides.

The Makepeace Experiment is an antihistorical novel, but one must distinguish between two visions of history, just as the Symbolist poet Alexander Blok distinguished between two visions of time. According to the first, history is concerned with chronology, changes in the spheres of politics, economics, technology, and those favoring such a view tend toward a progress-oriented or teleological vision.

According to the second, history is mainly connected with the life of the people, with culture in its broadest, most anthropological sense, including art, myth, religion, and everything from children's riddles to the manner in which the dead are buried; politics, reasons of state, progress are alien, and what is emphasized here is the permanent and the cyclical. Russian history clearly partakes of both, and Sinyavsky plays them off against each other, showing results both tragic and comic; tragic because historic changes willed by certain leaders in Russia have usually met with the stubborn, conservative resistance of the people and thus have had to be imposed by force and violence; comic because the passive strength of the people often absorbs, transforms, and outlives the intrusions of their rulers without losing its own specific character and identity, and that is precisely the "joke" of *The Makepeace Experiment*.

The theme of this novel is, as we have seen, quite simple, but its presentation is not. The success or failure of a *roman à thèse* depends upon how well it identifies people with ideas; if they remain recognizably separate entities, one is left with an allegory that is likely to be tendentious, predictable, hollow. But if the drama proves the thesis by embodying it and playing out its implications, the illusion of fiction gives life to the idea. In *War and Peace* the antiheroic organic vision of history is vindicated, not by the epilogue, but by the fates of the characters, which of course Tolstoy has arranged so that we view them as he wants us to. Sinyavsky has chosen to decorate and elaborate his narrative with designs from Russian literature, both oral and written, with Russian customs and superstitions, and traits of the national character as he sees it, so that the mightiest presence in the tale is the Russian people. But the tale has its dialectical side: although Tikhomirov, who would create paradise on earth and perfect man, is opposed to the powerful inertia of the Russian people, he is not alien to it; rather, the inertia calls him into being; he is its antithesis, the impatient idealist driven by the force of his own will and vision to elevate his people who, left to themselves would slip out of history entirely and merely continue to live from generation to generation.

The plot itself fixes on Leonid Tikhomirov, a bicycle mechanic, who learns the secret of mass hypnosis from an old book dropped on him by his long dead ancestor Proferansov, a Russian intellectual and aristocrat, who haunts both the plot and the narrator. Tikhomirov creates an illusory utopia by hypnotizing the inhabitants of Lyubimov in order to win the love of a sophisticated Jewess, Serafima Petrovna; she deserts him in the end when his dedication to social progress eclipses their love, and soon thereafter Tikhomirov loses the power to project his will through space. The town is retaken by robot tanks, Tikhomirov jumps on a box car, Lyubimov returns to its time-honored ways, and another episode of Russian history has come to a close with no permanent traces left on the life of the people, bringing to mind Chaadaev's tirades about the nonhistorical nature of the Russians and Sinyavsky's own, more approving, comments on this subject in *Thought Unaware*. The erotic motif should be seen metaphorically, exactly in the spirit

employed by Sinyavsky when discussing political-erotic
symbolism in *On Socialist Realism,* and not viewed as an
unmasking of the historical principle as it is, for example,
in the modern Polish novel *The Gates of Paradise (Bramy
raju)*, by Jerzy Andrzejewski, where a web of sexual relationships is shown to be the motive force of a medieval
children's crusade. Rather, Serafima as a Jew represents the
soul of history which calls men to great deeds, a fickle Clio
whose Jewishness provides the Russian narrator an opportunity to reveal his ambivalent feelings about Jews:

I know the toughness there is in that Jewish race which is
scattered over the face of the earth like raisins in a pudding or
pepper in a stew—but not like salt, because salt dissolves
whereas the Jews keep their original properties, the ones God
endowed them with. And perhaps the reason He scattered
them throughout the world is for them to show their toughness and enduring obstinacy, and for us—when we come across
them in the middle of our Russian stew—to remember that
history didn't begin today and that no one can tell how it will
end.[1]

From the very outset her role as an agent of history is
established, but it should be noted that the humorously
vulgar culinary metaphors in which this rather abstract
thought is couched bring the thought back down to earth
in a hurry, a trick Sinyavsky learned from Gogol and
Rozanov.

In his previous writings Sinyavsky frequently alluded to
the great works of Russian literature, playing with them,
distorting them for comic purposes, paying homage to

past masters. In *The Makepeace Experiment* he incorporates lines from Russian literature directly into the text. Since the novel is really a human fable, a fairy tale of Russian history, which compresses time and space into one short period in one little Russian town, the characters are archetypal, and though they speak a very current Soviet idiom, their conversation sometimes includes lines of Russian poetry spoken, of course, without regard for time. Thus, for example, when Samson Samsonovich Proferansov returns from his voyage to India (sometime in the nineteenth century) he greets his old nurse, Arina Rodionovna (who just happens to bear the same name as Pushkin's famous nanny), with the opening lines of Sergei Yesenin's poem "A Letter to My Mother," written in 1924:

> Hey, my old lady, still alive?
> Me too. Greetings to you, greetings! [2]

The opening chapter, in which Leonid Tikhomirov takes control of the town of Lyubimov, derives its humor from the playing off of ancient elements of Russian culture against the banal celebration of May Day in a provincial town. In their struggle for power Tikhomirov and the man he challenges, Tishchenko, continually transform themselves from one beast to another, as commonly happens in Russian fairy tales (*skazki*) and in the well-known seventeenth-century poem "Misery-Luckless-Plight" ("Gore-Zloschastie"). Traditional metamorphosis is given a modern, satirical touch; Tishchenko, while being pursued as a crow by Tikhomirov in the guise of a borzoi, turns into a

bicycle, whereupon Tikhomirov turns himself into a motorcycle. This joke, which is very much in harmony with the
general theme of the novel, works two ways, for the modern elements (bicycle, motorcycle) both clash and accord
with the past and the traditional animal symbolism. There
may be progress in technology, but the uses to which it is
put never change.

The opening chapter also formulates people's history in
terms of drinking and speeches:

Ours was to listen to Comrade Tishchenko and drink after-
wards. We weren't alcoholics, we could wait, it's never too
late for a drink if you have the money. After Comrade Tishchenko's speech, there was nothing to stop us from drinking
for the rest of the day.[3]

The theme of drinking runs throughout the entire novel
just as it runs throughout Russian history (one of the
earliest Slavic writings describes the Russians as being unable to live without drinking).[4] But drinking should not be
viewed only from the social standpoint as a "problem." In
Thought Unaware, Sinyavsky treats vodka as a sort of
Slavic psychedelic, liberating the imagination from the
world, as opposed to sex, which he calls "black magic" and
which, as we have already seen in the development of *The
Makepeace Experiment*'s plot, causes trouble. The specific
mystical character of Russian drinking is apostrophized as a
means of rising above matter and feeling fully free and
alive:

And what's the use of freedom to a Russian if he is not to
have his fling and enjoy himself to the damnation of his soul,

the terror of his enemies, and for something to remember at the hour of his death?

We Russians are not fond of tippling amateurishly, in solitude, each in his corner, a teaspoonful at a time. We leave this kind of thing to foreigners, to Americans in America and Frenchmen in France, drunkards who drink in order to befuddle their brains and then to sleep it off like pigs. What we drink for is to fire our souls and to feel we are alive. It's when we drink that we come to life, our spirit rises about inert matter and soars into the empyrean—and what we need for this exercise is a street, a crooked small-town street with its hump rising into the white sky.[5]

Sinyavsky is stressing the mystical nature of Russian drunkenness and its specific national character as well. When pressed on this point at his trial, he responded:

What I value most of all in my fellow Russians is their inner spiritual freedom and what one might call their fantasy, which manifests itself both at the sublime level of the gift to the world of Dostoevsky, in their art and songs, and also at a more humble, everyday level. But it does not seem to me that we have to praise the Russian people at every end and turn, even though I regard them as the greatest people on earth.[6]

And here, in the author's own words, spoken in his own defense, is a perfect summary of the theme of *The Makepeace Experiment.*

Just as he refused to idealize the Russian people, Sinyavsky refused to idealize the Russian landscape as so many works of Socialist Realism do, with their golden oceans of rye and gleaming tractors. His characterization of Russian nature is somewhat reminiscent, in its pathos, of Tiutchev's Slavophile landscape:

These poor villages,
this humble landscape—
native land of long suffering,
land of the Russian people!

The foreigner's haughty glance
will not understand or notice
what shines mysteriously
through your humble nakedness.

Weighed down by the burden of the cross,
the King of Heaven, in a servant's guise,
has walked all over you,
blessing you, my native land.[7]

But Sinyavsky's landscape does not possess such dramatic intensity, rather its every detail is charged with quizzical affection and humor:

White tablecloths, red flags and purple skirts billowed in the wind, clashing with the tender green of the young fields running their wedges from the skyline into the valley and cutting across the bare, steely-looking woods. Add to this the winding, branching, bottle-colored river, the townsfolk clustering along its banks, the narrow, twisting streets and alleys and the lopsided church with crows wheeling around its broken dome; the graveyard like a sampler in a faded cross-stitch, the yellow hospital shaped like a coffin and, next to it, the brownish-red rectangular block of the prison; add the waste plot with its mounds of rubbish and the empty highway streaked silver with mud, the belfry, the fences, the scuffling dogs, the wail of a concertina, the curl of smoke rising from a chimney and the clouds racing like horses with flowing manes—add and mix, and you will have the picture which lay before the eyes of Makepeace and his suite.[8]

Though the two writers may share similar Slavophile sentiments, Sinyavsky scrupulously avoids the hieratic tone of
Tiutchev, if only because he knows that it has been usurped
by rulers; in fact, he puts such lofty sentiments in Tikhomirov's mouth, giving them a comic twist for good measure: " 'Behold the fulfillment of the people's century-old
dream. Behold the rivers of milk and honey, the Kingdom
of Heaven which in scientific terms is the great leap forward!' " [9] Sinyavsky describes landscape with the same
benign whimsy with which Chagall has depicted his native
town of Vitebsk, and Alfreda Aucouturier notes that
"when he [Sinyavsky] learned that the wrapper of the
Italian edition [of *The Makepeace Experiment*] carried a
picture by Chagall, he was very moved to realize that he
had been so well understood." [10]

Undoubtedly the novel was inspired in part by Sinyavsky's
travels to the north of Russia and in particular to the village
of Denkovo, where he discovered the age-old traditions of
Russian life calmly continuing in the midst of modern
Soviet society. The English edition of *On Trial* contains
several of the photographs the Sinyavskys took of the
people, costumes, and landscape of this region, and these
photographs are worth examining in conjunction with reading *The Makepeace Experiment*.

In his essay "Man without an Adjective," Gregory
Pomerants writes:

Recently, a Muscovite girl, a specialist in folklore, was getting
married. The bridesmaids, together with the bride, performed
the Vologda wedding ritual. The guests were trying hard to
live up to their archaic roles, and the *tysiatsky*, master of cere-

monies (incidentally, he was a Jew), was doing it rather artistically. But everything was just a game. The old Vologda village, where any other way of celebrating a wedding would have been unthinkable, and the ritual carried on by old women through many centuries, became as exotic as Tahiti. Had the girls studied African culture, they would have danced to the beat of tom-toms, while the students of Indian culture would have performed the dances of Krishna. . . . What was once something real, a thing of vital importance, becomes a game, one of many games that may be played. . . . We eat bread harvested by people whom we by force of habit call "peasants," but we do not live in a peasant society; we are no longer surrounded by the *narod*, "the peasantry." [11]

Something of this no doubt applies to Sinyavsky, for he is, to some degree, the city-dweller and intellectual struck by his discovery of his people. But this is not a work of "enthusiasm" and idealization, but a vision of history expressed in the language of fable and beloved cliché, and it radiates the serenity of contemplations achieved after much inner struggle; it is an archaeology of the Russian spirit, and the ghost Proferansov provides the clue for this interpretation: "If you want to explain the intricacies of Russian history, you have to write in layers. You remember the excavations at the monastery—how the various strata were uncovered in their chronological order?—eighteenth-century shoe soles, sixteenth-century shards and so on? Well, it's the same thing with writing. You obviously can't keep on always excavating at the same level." [12] When traditional Russian customs are placed side by side with Soviet motifs for satirical effect, as when, taking power, Tikhomirov

bows to the four corners of the earth and then requests no
personality cult be built up around him, these elements do
not really exist side by side except in the linear progression
of the narrative; they are, in fact, meant to be held simul-
taneously in the reader's mind and seen in transparent
layers, one on top of the other.

Fantastic elements of the collective imagination are galvan-
ized by Tikhomirov's actions—some see him as Christ,
others as anti-Christ, while still others view him as the just
Tsar for whom Russia has been waiting for centuries, a
Tsar who may be easily approached and who will listen to
his people's troubles. When Tikhomirov projects his hypnotic will into space, Lyubimov is rendered invisible, like
the legendary city of Kitezh. Two women, Serafima, the
soul of history, and Tikhomirov's mother, the soul of the
people and the symbol of the abiding reality of daily life,
struggle for Tikhomirov's heart. The mother has no concern for historical greatness, rather, she worries constantly
about her son's health, and most of her dialogue is confined
to asking him if he would like some cottage cheese or sour
cream. Her instincts are entirely conservative—to protect,
maintain, nourish. She is something of a stock-in-trade figure,
appropriate to a fairy tale. It must be remembered that this
is a fairy tale where, as the narrator remarks, "everything
is large and kindly," where clichés come alive redeemed by
a vision of love, in this respect resembling the Polish epic
Pan Tadeusz by Adam Mickiewicz. Sinyavsky's satire does
not fall exclusively onto things Soviet; Russian superstition
and religious blindness are also satirized, and when Tikho-

mirov, at his wedding, turns the river into Soviet cham-
pagne, this is as much a parody of the wedding at Cana as
an echo of Adam Ważyk's well-known "Poem for Adults"
(1955):

> Fourier, the dreamer, charmingly foretold
> that lemonade would flow in seas.
> Does it flow?
> They drink sea water,
> crying:
> "lemonade!"
> returning home secretly
> to vomit.[13]

In the end, the works of "history" are looked upon with
amused contempt and wry humor; as usual, they have come
to naught:

Here was the site of the Stadium—one ditch had been dug and
half the monastery wall demolished for bricks; over there were
the foundations of the Matrimonial Palace with its Fountain of
Love, planned in honor of the traitor and embezzler of today;
and further along the Avenue, still hidden by the mists of the
future, were the projected Palaces of Science, Youth, Labor,
Realistic Art, and a small and unassuming Palace of Bicycle
Production and Repairs.

Among these unfinished monuments and unplanted gardens,
children were playing in the dust and rubble, while a peasant,
calm and morose, pissed unashamedly into a concrete mixer
half full of cement.[14]

Though this passage has definite satirical application to the
Soviet scene, it has wider implications as well—disgust with
the whole notion of great historical enterprise (when it

does not arise from the real needs of human beings) and faith in man, with a realistic appreciation of his faults and his worth. In every vision of a glorious future there is a hidden contempt for man as he is.

Disgust with history is not a view peculiar to Sinyavsky. Though Andrei Amalrik disagrees with him on many points, on this essential one they are close; Amalrik's *Will the Soviet Union Survive until 1984?* concludes with these words:

Meanwhile, we are told, Western prognosticators are indeed worried by the growth of the cities and the difficulties brought on by the rapid pace of scientific and technological progress. Evidently, if "futurology" had existed in Imperial Rome, where, as we are told, people were already erecting six-story buildings and children's merry-go-rounds were driven by steam, the fifth-century "futurologists" would have predicted for the following century the construction of twenty-story buildings and the industrial utilization of steam power.

As we now know, however, in the sixth century goats were grazing in the Forum—just as they are doing now, beneath my window, in this village.[15]

The Makepeace Experiment and Sinyavsky's first novel, *The Trial Begins*, have many similarities—the reappearance of the twin secret policemen Tolya and Vitya, the theme of thought detection, the paranoia of the narrator ("Any moment there will be a new wave of arrests. If they search the house and find the manuscript under the floorboards, they'll pick up every single one of us"). There are so many similarities that, in fact, the former can be seen as something of a rewrite of the latter. No doubt, as Sinyavsky's own excavation of himself progressed, he realized the flaws of *The Trial Begins,* chief among them the vacillating tone and point of view that make it a spiritually and aesthetically fragmented work held together primarily by the mechanics of the plot. Having found a deeper and steadier way of looking at himself, history, and the world, he again attempted to write a historical tale. But this time, rather than sticking close to specific events, he confronted Russian history on the level of its fundamental conflict, that between the sane inertia of the people and the tragic-comic imperatives of its leaders. Dealing with this dialectic he succeeded in creating a unity of tone, vision, and action. *The Makepeace Experiment* thus closes the cycle begun in 1956 with the writing of *On Socialist Realism* and *The Trial Begins.* The new art Sinyavsky called for to explore the mysteries of a new age could not have been created except by quest and experiment, and by greater understanding of himself, his time and country. The success of Sinyavsky's venture reminds us that though talent is indispensable, it does not guarantee the achievement known as art, and that the maturing of the author's spirit and character alone can provide the timbre of unique authority that compels attention and respect.

8

Sinyavsky as a Critic

The works of fiction and nonfiction that Sinyavsky published under the pen name of Tertz betray common origins, common preoccupations, and a continuous process of cross-fertilization. But when the critical works of Sinyavsky published in the Soviet Union are compared with the works of Tertz, a sharp contrast emerges, not so much in the substance or concern of the works as in the constricted contours of the former, reflecting the conditions under which they were written, the taboos they had to confront. The criticism published in the Soviet Union is often cramped into caution by the pressures every Soviet writer brings to his desk.

Toward the end of his examination at his trial, Sinyavsky remarked:

"In my articles (in the Soviet press) I was giving not only my own views but also the views of the editors who commissioned them. . . . I have been attacked and quite a lot was done to stop me publishing what I wanted to. . . . I do not regard my works published abroad as anti-Soviet. And I do not think they differ basically from what I have published here." [1]

The key word here is "basically." Although Sinyavsky admits that his criticism published in the Soviet Union was

distorted by external pressures, he maintains that he was not
leading a double life, not double-dealing, but rather playing
the same impulse in two directions, one against the difficult
odds of Soviet society, the other in the free space of the
imagination, where there is great but subtle pressure to be
true. The degree of distortion is often directly proportional
to the nature of the publication for which he is writing. His
articles for *The History of Soviet Russian Literature*
(*Istoriya russkoy sovetskoy literatury*), for example, are
very standard stuff with only faint glimmers of the intelligence behind them, whereas those he wrote for Tvardov-
sky's liberal *Novy mir* frequently reflect his wit, style, and
manner. The comment of Laszlo Tikos and Murray Peppard in their introduction to *For Freedom of the Imagination* (a collection of Sinyavsky's criticism in English translation) is a bit off the mark:

Andrei Sinyavsky followed a well-established literary tradition
in Russia: he was active not only as a writer of fiction but also
as a literary critic. From Pushkin to Marina Tsvetayeva, from
Dostoevsky to Andrei Sinyavsky, creative artists in Russia
often combined creative work with theoretical studies on the
problems of their craft.[2]

When he was forced by circumstance and character into
the Sinyavsky-Tertz relationship, Sinyavsky was hardly
following a traditional route.

Any discussion of Sinyavsky as a critic must take into
account the fact that some of his most important work in
this area was done in collaboration with other writers. Any

two men able to write together must hold views that are compatible almost to the point of being identical, or at least are close enough together to make every compromise an accord. For that reason, any views which appear in an article coauthored by Sinyavsky can be ascribed to him with some degree of assurance, but never with complete assurance or finality unless they are also found in other works written by him alone.

In all there are twenty pieces of literary criticism associated with Sinyavsky's name.[3] Nineteen of them were published in the Soviet Union, and only one, his essay on Yevtushenko, "In Defense of the Pyramid" ("V zashchitu piramidy"), was published abroad in the Russian émigré journal *Grani* in Munich in 1967, after having been written for *Novy mir* and rejected by it shortly before his arrest. His critical writings can, and probably should, be classified according to the publications in which they appeared. Sinyavsky published three articles in *The History of Soviet Russian Literature*, one on Gorky, one on Bagritsky, and a third on the literature of World War II. His principal outlet for his critical articles and reviews was the journal *Novy mir*, where he published nine pieces during 1959–1965. These articles, in which we see Sinyavsky operating with the most scope and the least distortion, show his preference for poets (articles on Anna Akhmatova, Olga Bergholtz, Pasternak, Robert Frost), his ability to devastate politely (in his articles on Shevtsov, Sofronov, and Dolmatovsky, hacks and "politicians" of literature), and his polemical talents as well. The concern with science fiction and the fantastic evidenced in "Pkhentz" and "The Icicle" took critical shape as well in two article-reviews: "Bez skidok ("No Discount") appeared in *Voprosy literatury* in 1960, and "Realizm fantasiki" ("The Realism of the Fantastic") appeared in *Literaturnaya gazeta* in the same year. One of his critical pieces, a short study of Babel, is to be found only in French, in *Oeuvres et Opinions*, a magazine published by the Union of Soviet Writers. This study is probably an offshoot of the longer study of Babel on which he was known to be working, and which had been the source of considerable trouble, as he complained at his trial. Further, there is his long introduction to the 1965 edition of Pasternak's poetry and narrative poems (*Stikhotvoreniya i poemy*), a long book (440 pages) entitled *The Poetry of the First Years of the Revolution 1917–1920* (*Poeziya pervykh let revolyutsii 1917–1920*)published in 1964 and written in collaboration with A. Menshutin, and a pamphlet on Picasso written in collaboration with his friend, the art historian Igor Naumovich Golomshtok.

The reader of Sinyavsky's three articles in *The History of Soviet Russian Literature* is unlikely to find out very much about the author or his subjects. Writing for such an "official" publication and on such sacrosanct subjects as Gorky and the literature of the Second World War, Sinyavsky has been able to do little more than categorize the genres begun by Gorky and others which flourished during the war. Since Gorky is the father of Socialist Realism (about which *On Socialist Realism* comments, "a senile fancy of Gorky's?"), his stature puts him beyond the reach of literary critics, who are reduced to repeating hagiographic formulae:

Gorky's creative work has acquired such exceptional significance in the life of society and in the literature of the twentieth century precisely because it contained the fullest and most truthful reflection of the most important phenomenon of the epoch—the revolutionary struggle of the working class.[4]

This definition is reminiscent of a statement of the Hungarian Marxist critic Georg Lukács, who holds that greatness is related not to talent or genius for humanity, but to being in tune with the age: "Gorky is a great writer—and a great writer measured by the standards of the great realistic classics—because he saw and depicted every aspect of the revolutionary crisis."[5] Much of the section on Gorky is devoted to his unfinished novel *Klim Samgin*, which was the subject of Sinyavsky's dissertation (accepted in 1952, never published), and Sinyavsky doubtless drew on it for this article. Characteristic of the approach that Sinyavsky takes here is his interpretation of fictional characters totally in social terms, of whole novels as actual parts of the social process. Sinyavsky goes so far as to say that the works *Mother* (*Mat'*) and *Enemies* (*Vragi*) are necessarily unfinished because they were written before the Great October Revolution, which would have provided them their logical social and literary climax. Nowhere is there a hint that Gorky's writings in any genre, from publicistic articles to novels, are anything less than exemplary, and only in Sinyavsky's extra praise for Gorky's autobiography and memoirs is there a subtle criticism of the prose fiction. Perhaps the following outburst from *On Socialist Realism* not only satirizes the follies and excesses of Gorky but settles an old score as well, restoring with a burst of mockery a balance upset by years of obligatory praise:

Gorky roared "NO!" at these superfluous men, who roused his ire by their indefiniteness, and called them "petty bourgeois." Later he extended the concept of "petty bourgeois" far and wide and cast into it all who did not belong to the new religion: property owners large and small, liberals, conservatives, hooligans, humanists, decadents, Christians, Dostoevsky, Tolstoy.[6]

Sinyavsky's treatment of the Russian literature of the Second World War, the opening article of the third volume of *The History of Soviet Literature*, is forty-eight pages long, some twenty pages shorter than the piece on Gorky. Because of the limited space (whatever the reason behind it), the topic itself, and the official nature of the publication, in this article Sinyavsky has little opportunity to explore one of his favorite subjects, the repercussions in literature of a great historical shock, which he examines at length and in detail in his book *The Poetry of the First Years of the Revolution 1917–1920*. Here he traces the resurgence of national self-consciousness, the reappearance of the sketch and publicistic writing, the simplifying of artistic language so that words, accessible to all, could be found for the common ordeal, and he says that Soviet poetry experienced a genuine flowering in the years 1941–1945. Of the publicistic character of the prose of the period he writes: "If the artistic literature of the war years is publicistic, propagandistic, then the publicistic works of this period are—artistic." [7] He divides wartime prose fiction into two categories: the first is the romantic-heroic, represented by Boris Gorbatov's *Nepokorennye* ("The Unbowed"); the second includes the works marked by restraint, simplicity, and matter-of-factness, for example, Konstantin Simonov's *Dni i nochi* (*Days and Nights*). On the whole this article shows that Sinyavsky was well able to manipulate the canonical motifs of Soviet literary criticism, and it may have provided him with the ammunition of respectability in the bitter infighting that characterizes the Soviet literary scene. Sinyavsky is clearly more at home in his short sketch of the literary career of the poet Eduard Bagritsky (1895–1934), whose evolution as a Romantic he characterizes as follows: "The move from literature to life, from bookish romanticism to a romantic understanding of actual reality—this is Bagritsky's creative path." [8] In *On Socialist Realism,* as well as in his critical articles published in the Soviet Union, Sinyavsky sharply differentiates between a bookish, melancholic, escapist Romanticism and one whose breadth, extravagance, and élan are in accord with a mighty historical event, a reality itself romantic. A romantic period, according to Sinyavsky, is a time in which the human spirit rises collectively to struggle against the forces of oppression, and he characterizes the Second World War as romantic in this sense, close in many respects to the Civil War.

The sketch of Bagritsky shows how Bagritsky's changing poetics mirrors his spiritual evolution, a movement from disembodied exaltations to an exaltation of the earth, the common, the ordinary, which coincides with his movement toward accepting the Revolution and its consequences. Of the three articles in *The History of Soviet Russian Literature* (*HSRL*), the study of Bagritsky alone is both recognizably Sinyavsky's own and able to stand as a useful and perceptive piece of literary criticism.

The play of Sinyavsky's personality is most evident in the nine articles he wrote for *Novy mir*. Three of these articles were coauthored by A. Menshutin, whose studies of Fedin and Mayakovsky can be found in *HSRL*, in the same volumes as Sinyavsky's. Menshutin, a colleague of Sinyavsky at the Gorky Institute of World Literature, was also coauthor of the book *The Poetry of the First Years of the Revolution 1917–1920*, and with the artist N. Kishilov he wrote a strongly worded letter of protest to the editors of *Literaturnaya gazeta* after that paper had published Kedrina's attack ("The Heirs of Smerdyakov") on Daniel and Sinyavsky. The first article by Sinyavsky and Menshutin, "Russian Poetry Day" ("Den' russkoy poezii"), appeared in *Novy mir* early in 1959. In it, they gently chide the superpatriots for confusing good taste with commendable sentiments. They employ wry understatement when reviewing the following lines: "kak samye luchshie / glavy romana / chitaetsya skromanya svodka / Gosplana" ("The modest summary / of the Five Year Plan / reads like the finest / chapters of a novel"). They write:

Though fundamentally correct, this declaration conceals the danger of a somewhat oversimplified understanding of the tasks of art.[9]

This article is also noteworthy for its criticism of Voznes-ensky's fascination with flashy effects and word games, and it warns of their danger for his future development. The work of young Soviet poets is further analyzed in "In Favor of Poetic Activity" ("Za poeticheskuyu aktivnost'," *Novy mir*, January 1961), with slightly pessimistic con-clusions drawn as to the abilities and futures of the new generation of poets. This article provoked great contro-versy. Six pieces attacking it appeared within a few months, and the authors responded to these in August of the same year in the article "Let's Talk Professionally" ("Davayte govorit' professional'no"). Although they do not number themselves among the fans of Voznesensky, Sinyavsky and Menshutin feel called upon to defend him against charges of misanthropy and pornography; agreeing that Voznesen-sky writes of the dark sides of life, they counter the attack on him and themselves:

The duty of the Soviet poet, above all else, is to see "the darkest stains" in reality and to bravely go out to battle them, burning these stains out of our life by means of artistic exposure.[10]

They also defend their assessments of poets whose "work biographies" are impeccable, but who, unfortunately, write bad poetry. The six-article attack occasioned a defense of Sinyavsky and Menshutin by the editorial board, which follows their article in that issue.

His other *Novy mir* pieces show Sinyavsky in a variety of roles: "rehabilitating" poets by clarifying and defending their works (Olga Bergholtz, Anna Akhmatova—into the essay on whom he slips lines from her long poem, *Requiem*, never published in the Soviet Union); attacking his enemies (Dolmatovsky, Sofronov, Shevtsov, whom he considers the enemies of Russian literature); reviewing a new collection of translations of Robert Frost's poetry, which he describes in much the same terms he applies to Pasternak's viewing it as a poetry that affirms the unity of all things. Among these pieces there is also a brief notice on Pasternak's collected poems (*Poeticheskiy sbornik*, 1961) in which Sinyavsky complains about the absence of several important poems and calls for a separate edition of Pasternak's translations, which seemed to have been used in this volume to crowd out the more controversial poems. But Pasternak is treated in much greater detail by Sinyavsky in his introduction to the 1965 edition of Pasternak's poetry.

Sinyavsky's review of Yevtushenko's "Bratsk Hydroelectric Station" ("Bratskaya GES," 1965) was rejected in that same year by *Novy mir* and was published two years later in the Russian émigré publication *Grani* in Germany. Sinyavsky, in this essay entitled "In Defense of the Pyramid" ("V zashchitu piramidy"), is extremely severe toward Yevtushenko and judges him by the very standards —"to the heights, to the depths!" ("vvys' i vglub!")—that Yevtushenko pretends to apply to himself. Sinyavsky mocks Yevtushenko's "illusion of significance," his coarsening of history, his confusion of imagery and, in the end, finds Yevtushenko's central fault to be one of character and spirit, the lack of a genuine identity and genuine commitment. We can see how high Sinyavsky holds the vocation of the poet when, in the following remarks, he measures Yevtushenko by its standards:

Yevtushenko, for all his proneness to self-display, lacks the stamp of an exclusive personality, the idea of a vocation, or of a great and terrible fate which would impart to the poet's destiny something providential and not to be resisted, and at the same time would allow him to develop his own biography like a legend, in which personal life is raised to the level of a unique saga, half real, half invented, and created day by day before an astonished public.[11]

In his criticism Sinyavsky constantly argues for a higher level of taste and higher literary standards, but his point of view is by no means purely aesthetic; rather, he sees a direct connection between technical sophistication and the appreciation of the complexity of reality. He is continually struggling for greater freedom of intellectual inquiry, and he bases this struggle not on an appeal to the rights of man but on the fantastic, complex, and mysterious nature of reality itself, which refuses to yield to the crude tools of ideology, doctrine, and orthodoxy. This sense of mysterious complexity is the moving force and the basic educative impulse behind all his criticism, and is present both when he attacks and defends, when he illuminates or chides.

Himself a proponent of science fiction as a serious literary genre, which he argues should be published in *Novy mir*, Sinyavsky, in his two reviews on science fiction, skir-

mishes with Soviet authors working in this genre who fear
to make their stories too fantastic. The human imagination,
he argues, must project itself across great distances, in every
sense of the word, simply because technology develops
with such velocity that today's fantasy is tomorrow's
obsolescence. Here again, Sinyavsky is taking a line similar
to that of Sakharov and the other liberal scientists who base
their appeal for greater freedom on the demonstrable complexity of the universe.

Sinyavsky's short sketch of Babel in *Oeuvres et opinions*
treats his major themes and his style, and pays homage to
him as a literary mastery from whom Sinyavsky learned not
only how to turn a phrase or fashion an image, but certain
fundamental artistic processes as well—how to shock, stimulate, excite, confuse, illuminate. Sinyavsky feels particularly close to Babel's romantic approach to reality, an
approach in which contrast, hyperbole, the grotesque are
used, not for sensational purposes, but to open the reader's
mind and force him deeper into reality. Speaking of Babel's
Red Cavalry (*Konarmiya*), he defines what is for him an
ideal artistic temperament: "The lucidity of the realist
does not cool the fiery temperament of the romantic." [12]
Such a temperament alone allows the artist to include and
unite in his work all the extremes and polarities of experience: "The moral and aesthetic grandeur of these men
though spotted with blood and mud. . . . The terrifying
is related gently, the sublime grossly." [13] In Babel, Sinyavsky sees not only a kindred artistic spirit but an ally in the
struggle against the primitive conception of realism:

But for Babel fiction is not the contrary of reality. The truth of fiction helps one to better penetrate the truth of life and to recreate it in a much more convincing fashion than can a vulgar copy. To "invent" is not to "trick." [14]

Like nearly all of Sinyavsky's literary heroes, Babel had suffered at the hands of the authorities, and Sinyavsky does not hesitate to mention that fact in this article: "In May 1939, Babel was illegally arrested and perished." [15]

In 1960, in collaboration with the art historian Igor Naumovich Golomshtok, Sinyavsky published a short, profusely illustrated brochure on Picasso, of which one hundred thousand copies were printed. Golomshtok, who was examined at Sinyavsky's trial, spoke highly of Sinyavsky's respect for, and commitment to, Russian culture, and he was reported to have received a suspended sentence of six months for refusing to name the people from whom he had acquired copies of Sinyavsky's fiction.

Given what we know of his background, it comes as no surprise that Sinyavsky wrote this booklet on Picasso. His wife studied art history, specialized in restoring ikons, and made jewelry. His fiction, while rejecting photographic realism, is nevertheless richly decorated with stylized visual images whose lyrical and grotesque distortions are somewhat in the manner of Chagall or the early Kandinsky. And, of course, in his call for a new art at the end of *On Socialist Realism*, Sinyavsky places Chagall and Goya in the family tree of fantastic realism. Though leaning more toward a mental than a sensual apprehension of life, Sinyavsky could never say of himself, as did Aldous Huxley:

"I am and, for as long as I can remember, I always have been a poor visualizer. Words, even the pregnant words of poets, do not evoke pictures in my mind." [16]

It was a happy day for the writers and artists of Eastern Europe when Pablo Picasso decided to join the Communist Party. In view of his prominence communist governments could no longer afford to identify modern art totally with the decadent capitalism of the West, an idea which has no basis in fact, since modernism has its Russian roots in Kandinsky, Tatlin, and the former Commissioner of Fine Arts for the town of Vitebsk, Marc Chagall. Only the death of Stalin, the subsequent Thaw, and Picasso's prestige made it possible for Picasso's paintings to be shown in the Soviet Union and for Sinyavsky's little book to be written.

The function of Sinyavsky and Golomshtok's brochure is primarily educative, and the brochure should be judged solely in the context of Russian society and culture, and not with regard to the vast literature on Picasso which has developed in the West. As well as introducing the work of a painter, Sinyavsky and Golomshtok must of necessity acculturate the reader-viewer's mind to properly perceive and understand the language of Picasso's art. The long years of Socialist Realism, both in painting and in literature, had conditioned Russians to a very literal sense of art. Thus the authors' primary task is to convince the reader that realism is not the only means of penetrating and depicting reality, and that modern painters are not madmen illustrating their lunacies, but rather are like mathematicians and scientists who explore new fields of reality by means of theories and formulae that contradict common sense. A good part of this brochure is dedicated to driving this point home: "In order to find the right approach to Picasso's work, one should first of all take into consideration that the task of the artists is not to give us a copy of the world around us in his art." [17] To facilitate their task, the authors stress the socially progressive side of Picasso's work (Guernica, the peace dove). The comments on the paintings and the various periods provide a clear and direct introduction, emphasizing form to be not an end in itself but a key to doors never before opened; in a definition that recalls Sinyavsky's remarks on Babel, the authors write: "But, on the whole, Picasso's art is not a withdrawal from reality, but its comprehension. He destroys nature's forms in order to better understand and depict the laws of their formation." [18] This brochure must be seen in the light of its immediate and also its long-terms goals. It first of all attempts to introduce a difficult modern painter to a public which having been deprived for thirty years of a tradition, needs to be taught the ABC's of modern art. By accomplishing the first goal, the brochure assures the accomplishment of the second, which is to improve the climate of tolerance by demonstrating that nonrealistic art, when it is bound by a commitment to the world, can be an instrument of discovery.

The long introductory essay to the 1965 edition of Pasternak's *Poetry and Narrative Poetry* (*Stikhotvoreniya i poemy*) is Sinyavsky's single best piece of literary criticism and one of the most illuminating expositions of Pasternak's poetry ever written. It examines in depth Pasternak's poetics and world-view, and shrinks from neither praise nor criticism. For Pasternak, a poet of the unity of the world, poetics and world-view are indivisible, his poetics *is* his world-view, and Sinyavsky's criticisms of it are based on what it excludes, for within it he finds nothing but harmony.

The source of Pasternak's poetry is wonder, a return to primal innocence of vision: "Wonder at the miracle of existence—this is the attitude in which we see Pasternak throughout, forever amazed and enchanted by his discovery that 'it's spring again.' " [19] But here Sinyavsky's admiration is tinged with irony. Pasternak survived as a man and a poet by focusing his imagination on the eternal (in itself hardly a fault):

His attitude to life and to reality was determined by abstract ideals of moral perfection and did not always answer the concrete historical situation. His work in the main is about life seen from the point of view of the 'eternal' categories of goodness, love and universal justice.[20]

But his nonintellectual, even antiintellectual approach to life made the tragic history of his people somewhat inaccessible to him, made him in a sense far-sighted, able to view the eternal verities more clearly than the immediate, human world. Sinyavsky is by no means alone in his opinion of Pasternak's shortcomings. Czeław Miłosz says of Yuri Zhivago in an article entitled "On Pasternak Soberly": "Yuri has an intuitive grasp of good and evil but is no more able to understand what is going on in Russia than a bee can analyze chemically the glass of a windowpane against which it is beating." [21]

Sinyavsky's critical insights into Pasternak's poetry are of the first order. Of the role of landscape in Pasternak's poetry he writes: "In Pasternak landscape is often not so much the object of a description as the subject of the action, the principal hero and the mover of events." [22] He demonstrates the phonic principles of Pasternak's verse, in which the movement of a poem arises from the associative similarities of certain sounds, thereby making unexpected connections between phenomena not otherwise related and, by making these connections, creating a sense of unity that transcends and defies logic. Metaphor, Sinyavsky shows, plays a similar role:

In Pasternak's verse the chief role of metaphor is to connect one thing to another. Instantly and dynamically it draws the separate parts of reality into a single whole, and thus embodies the great unity of the world, the interaction and interpenetration of phenomena.[23]

Certain weaknesses of vision and character ("Pasternak could not do without his writing table," [24] writes Nadezhda Mandelstam) flawed Pasternak's integrity and marred his relations with the human world around him, but his poetic testament which affirms the beauty and unity of the world continues to provide spiritual sustenance for those Russians who, like Sinyavsky himself, seek to transform their values by changing their basis from ideology to the unity of life itself.

Sinyavsky and Menshutin's magnum opus, *The Poetry*

of the First Years of the Revolution, 1917–1920 (Poeziya pervykh let revolyutsii, 1917–1920), sets itself the momentous task of tracing the impact of the Revolution and Civil War on Russian consciousness as specifically expressed in the poetry of those years. The spirit of Alexander Blok is apparent in the basic orientation of their work, in its effort to catch and analyze "the music of history." Though they view the relationship between history and art as one of mutual influence, the authors give pride of place to the great events themselves, without, however, relegating poetry to the role of a mere "passive reflection." But since Sinyavsky and Menshutin hold that the key poetic relationship to be that of the poetic consciousness to the historical drama of events, they necessarily dismiss those who were not in close touch with the revolutionary meaning of the years 1917–1920. Obviously, such an approach allows them to limit their vast subject and as well to sidestep the tricky question of talented poets with no politics or the wrong politics.

For Sinyavsky the years covered by this book, 1917–1920, glow with the violent fires of creation as Russia breaks out of historical orbit to become the sun of the future. The mythic significance of this period for him has already been demonstrated and discussed. There is no question that his passionate attachment to this time helped him to penetrate its essence and recreate its creative turmoil in his own imagination, but the obverse is also worth examining: How much does Sinyavsky's emotional investment in his personal "myth" of these years in distinction to pressures from without obstruct him in his role as a critic and historian in this book? For the Romanticism which Sinyavsky professed in *On Socialist Realism* is certainly present here as well: "The romanticism which held sway in the Soviet poetry of the first years of the Revolution was, one might say, a hyperbolization of the sense of reality." [25] Sinyavsky's romantic attitude toward the Revolution has earned him some criticism from his staunchest admirers. Leonid Vladimirov in his book *The Russians* writes in reference to a passage in *On Socialist Realism:* "Alas, it isn't romanticism which Andrei Sinyavsky manifests here. This most intelligent, educated, level-headed writer is a victim of that same disease—unconscious, involuntary hypocrisy." [26] Vladimirov contends that Sinyavsky's hypocrisy springs from his emotional denial of the logical identification of the socialist state (*sotsialisticheskoe gosudarstvo*) and Soviet power (*sovetskaya vlast'*),[27] or, in other words, from his refusal to accept the Revolution and its consequences as a single entity. Perhaps this refusal is the source of one of the few weaknesses in this study of the poetry of the first years of the Revolution: it treats the events of 1917–1920 in all their historical richness and complexity, but also as if the next forty years of Soviet history never existed. What may have seemed true in the specific context of that period looks radically different when viewed in a longer historical expanse. How much of this blind spot may be attributed to Sinyavsky's myth of the Revolution and how much to the inexorable necessities hemming in all Soviet writers is simply unknowable.

The book's chapter titles make clear the four separate but related approaches taken to the subject matter: (1) Tendencies and Groups; (2) Peculiarities of the Artistic Imagination of the Epoch; (3) The Lyric, The Narrative Poem, Agitgenre; (4) Problems of Poetic Language. The authors are particularly adept at tracing the influence of various poetic schools and currents on one another and make some unexpected finds:

If the images of the Acmeists seemed just "petty" to proletarian poets and if Futurism was too coarse and unintelligible for them, then the abstract lexicon of Symbolism, where practically all words were capitalized, often seemed in their eyes to correspond to the enormous magnitudes of the day. This, specifically, explains the popularity of Symbolist clichés in the revolutionary poetry of the years 1917–1920, which had a great need for "lofty," "elevated" language, but which sometimes was compelled to make do with artificial substitutes of illusory aesthetic value.[28]

They isolate the principal movements of the time, including Cosmicism (Kozmizm), which sought to embrace the whole solar system and worlds beyond in its revolutionary ardor: "Vozdvignem na kanalakh Marsa / Dvorets svobody Mirovoy, / Tam budet basnya Karla Marksa / Siyat' kak geyzer ognevoy." ("On the canals of Mars we will erect / a Palace of World Freedom. / There Karl Marx tower will shine / like a geyser of fire."[29] They also trace the glorification of work by the Proletkult poets, the "democratization" of the language of poetry, the use of industrial and rural motifs (in Yesenin and the other "peasant poets" as well). They argue terminology to prove that Yesenin was never an Imagist and that Mayakovsky's break with Futurism came very early and that from 1918 on he was using the words "Futurism" and "Communism" almost interchangeably.

Although nominally the subject of this book is a period and its poetry, three individual poets, Bedny, Mayakovsky, and Blok, are shown towering above the rest; Sinyavsky and Menshutin single them out as the great poets of the age, "Central figures in the development of Soviet poetry in the years 1917–1920," [30] and play them off against one another, Bedny–Mayakovsky, Mayakovsky–Blok, to better display the qualities of each. Bedny and Mayakovsky, for instance, are shown to be close to the new age as it unfolds instant by instant, possessed by the spirit of "rightnowness" (*siyu-minutnost'*):

For Mayakovsky and Bedny always to be contemporary, in touch with the day, not one step behind life was a standard, a necessity and an achievement of which they were proud and which they maintained and cultivated in their poetry.[31]

Bedny's significance derives from his closeness to the people, their language, their daily life and from his role as a "teacher." His style of agitprop poetry is compared favorably with Mayakovsky's; Bedny convinces by using familiar expressions and idioms (likened to *lyubki*—cheap, popular prints that tell a story), whereas Mayakovsky exclaims and exhorts in the style of posters (*plakatny stil'*), a comparison that finishes in these rather comic remarks on Mayakovsky's style:

His poetry is recited standing up (and not "sitting on the *zavalinka,*" as is characteristic of Bedny): "I rose from the table, radiant with joy . . . ," "At such times as these you rise and speak to the ages, to history, the universe. . . ." "Rising" is his number one "verbal gesture" to use A. N. Tolstoy's expression which suggested itself at a reading of Mayakovsky's poetry and which underscores its extraordinary quality, seriousness, and significance.[32]

Not only do Sinyavsky and Menshutin take a Blokian approach to the subject matter of their book, they view Blok as the one poet who truly heard and transcribed the music of the upheaval, and they call him "the last great poet of prerevolutionary Russia and the first poet of the new age." His poem "The Twelve" is the symbol of his rebirth as a man and a poet and is praised nearly without qualification: " 'The immortal poem' about the revolution appeared a few months after the October events: in January 1918 Blok wrote 'The Twelve.' "[33] The authors find Mayakovsky wanting when compared with either Blok or Bedny, but for different reasons. Bedny is close to the masses, whereas Blok is close to the spirit that had inspired those masses, awakened their pride and their rage. In "The Twelve" Blok's ego is purified of the old, and his voice becomes the voice of the age, whereas Mayakovsky's voice is always too painfully his own. Sinyavsky and Menshutin summarize that difference in the following formula: "Blok introduces the 'music of the revolution' into his poetry, Mayakovsky, out of his own poetry, makes the 'music of the revolution'."[34] Though Sinyavsky and Menshutin diminish Mayakovsky's stature somewhat, they by no means denigrate him or reduce him to the ranks; they still view him as a great and significant poet. Perhaps this reduction in his status should be seen as a reaction against the cult of Mayakovsky, which had been, as Pasternak wrote, "introduced forcibly, like potatoes under Catherine the Great." [35]

Sinyavsky and Menshutin take their own stand on the controversial image of Christ leading the detachment of twelve Red Guards at the end of the poem. Although, according to them, the poem's form, tone, and content entirely justify the image, they refuse to assign it a single, exact meaning, holding that "the essence of its meaning is undefinable." [36]

Sinyavsky's fiction is yet another source where his critical insights into literature may be found. His stories and two short novels reflect and also reflect on both Russian literature and the literature of other countries, but it is to the literature of his own country that Sinyavsky feels closest. His fiction echoes the voices of the masters of Russian literature, parodies them, plays with them, pays them homage, analyzes them, and keeps them alive in his own work and time.

Any judgment on the criticism Sinyavsky wrote under his own name must be tempered by a sense of the extremely limited conditions under which he had to work. Some of his articles probably represent the price he paid for survival in the world of Soviet letters. A certain portion of his criticism is valuable for the Western reader and a greater portion for the Soviet reader, but in wit, passion, and intensity of thought none of it can compare with *On Socialist Realism.* Defending his creative integrity at his trial, Sin-yavsky said: "The study of literature for me was not a mask, it is my life's work and there was always a close relationship between my work as a critic and my work as a writer." [37] This statement is certainly true, but it does not show the complexity of Sinyavsky's situation. It was all that Sinyavsky was unable to express as a critic and a man that fed the imagination of Tertz and in that sense his work as a critic is closely related to his work as a writer. But there is a great distance between what can occur in the free imagination and the Soviet press, a distance for which Sinyavsky, obviously, is not responsible. Thus, the distance between the work of Sinyavsky and that of Tertz reflects not on the author but on the society in which he lives and reminds us of the burden he has to carry for so long. The Sinyavsky-Tertz relationship clearly demonstrates that creativity requires freedom. That freedom need not be granted by the authorities but can be discovered by a man within himself and, once discovered, cannot be taken away short of destroying him.

9

Epilogue: Sinyavsky for Russia and for the West

Andrei Sinyavsky has returned from his years of forced labor, but not to Moscow, his native city, where he is no longer allowed to live. This second stage of his punishment, a constant reminder of the power of the authorities, prevents him from reestablishing contact with the people, sights, and spirit of the city which figures so directly in many of his works; though he never took his city as his theme, Moscow was present as an ambiance, a backdrop, a flavor in nearly everything he wrote. Russia is generous in providing its writers with subjects, and Sinyavsky returns with nearly seven years' experience of the labor-camp Russia that had appeared so often in his tales as a menacing certainty. Reports have reached the West that Sinyavsky has written a study of the age of Pushkin in the prison jargon of the Zeks. What Sinyavsky will contribute to the genre of prison and camp literature, now a leading artistic form in Russian literature, remains to be seen; it will not be the wry and logical understatement of Amalrik, the tragic pathos of Solzhenitsyn and Nadezhda Mandelstam, or the passionate outrage of Marchenko, but something uniquely his own, bearing the mark of his free and versatile imagination.

Unlike Dostoevsky, who went into exile as a young and unformed writer, and unlike Solzhenitsyn, who entered his eight years of punishment with literary ambitions but without experience, Sinyavsky, before he began serving his sentence, had written at least five works of enduring value, *On Socialist Realism*, "The Icicle," "Pkhentz," *Thought Unaware*, and *The Makepeace Experiment*. He had already freed his mind from the maze of illusions built into it by his society.

Sinyavsky did not long for acclaim. Rather, he wished only to speak to his contemporaries in his own voice, which was not permitted. Though his style is daring in the architecture of its flights and though it pioneers areas of the Russian experience and of his own imagination, one feels an almost Chekhovian modesty in Sinyavsky arising not so much out of reserve as from a loathing of arrogance and exaggerated self-importance. Perhaps Sinyavsky's deepest desire has been to belong—to something vast, alive, and basically good. His "Marxist education" trained him to believe he was a soldier on the winning side in the war of history and provided him with a complex structure of myths and theories to support this conviction; in time, both his mind and his heart rebelled against that education. And yet, perhaps, communist ideology working in tandem with the traditional Russian sense of the collective prepared Sinyavsky for some of the steps on his path; as has been shown, communism has, both as a doctrine and in practice,

certain similarities with Christianity and religion in general
and thus promotes in its faithful a cruder version of the
religious world-view; furthermore, Soviet communism has
ruined traditional Christianity by destroying the churches,
scattering the priests, and annihilating dogma with science
and thus paradoxically it forces its own rebels into the
desert where true religion is born, where man and God are
alone together.

Setting out on his search, Sinyavsky knew that, after
communism, there would be no other total philosophy in
which to take shelter. Whatever he found, fought for,
created would be his own and that would have to suffice.
There would be nothing else. And he found that man,
fallen man, is sufficient to himself because he belongs at once
both to life, homely, familiar, tragicomic, and to the mystery of existence, to which he is bound by his mortality and
his imagination. In a certain sense the world is becoming
uniform in its faithlessness—all doctrine, all dogma, all
systems have lost their hypnotic charm and are revealed as
no more than attempts to deal with an overwhelming
world. At first this discovery can produce despair, cyni-
cism, nihilism, but, in the end, for those who do not stumble
or accept easy consolations, there is a liberation previously
unknown to man which marks a new stage in his maturity;
unsupported by any total faith, man must learn to be himself, to live, to find strength, peace, and hope in himself and
not turn like a child to leaders and priests. This Sinyavsky
has done.

His thought, his writing, and his life put Sinyavsky in

the avant-garde of both literature and humanity. His satire, unlike that of the absurdists of the West, has strong and healthy roots. Treated worse by fate than they, Sinyavsky preserves a love for the very creature, man, for his ways, his sorrows, his foolishness. Whereas Western writers too often deform and taunt, Sinyavsky has created an artistic vision of the world which proceeds from mystical wonder and which satirizes human follies and cruelties against that background. Whereas many artists in the West pervert their liberty at the whim of a malaise they are unable to shake and seem intent on robbing art of its seriousness, Sinyavsky envisioned a new form of art that would grasp the sinister grandeur of our age without succumbing to its lethal rootlessness, despair, intellectual vandalism, and by patient, solitary labor realized that vision in his work.

Sinyavsky's writings were done as an act of service. Russian literature had been mutilated by the pressures of the state, by threats, coercion, and murder, and his generation had inherited an abyss in their cultural history, a silence of nearly twenty-five years in their common past. As after a natural disaster people slowly return to their homes and begin to piece their lives together again, Sinyavsky reached back to the writers of the twenties, the Silver Age, and the nineteenth century to weave their voices into the music of his own time. That Sinyavsky sometimes regards the twenties too uncritically, that he occasionally makes excessive use of allusions to the Russian literature of the past, should be viewed in the context of what he was attempting, and not only as philosophic or literary flaws.

The literature that flowered so suddenly in Russia after 1956 has astounded the world with its scope, its depth, and its genius for humanity. Pasternak's *Doctor Zhivago*, Solzhenitsyn's novels and stories, the works of Sinyavsky, Nadezhda Mandelstam's *Hope against Hope*, the poetry of Brodsky, the social analysis of Amalrik, all bespeak a true rebirth of Russian culture. The origins of genius are unknown, and why talents should congregate in a particular place at a particular time is equally obscure, but in the case of present-day Russia some factors seem evident. The leeway created in the post-Stalin period produced a climate in which thought, while remaining hazardous, became possible again. The traditions of Russian literature demand moral seriousness and responsibility from the artist, whose province it is to express all that cannot otherwise find expression, all that is closest to man; the revival of these traditions, like a command from an officer, activated a whole series of writers, and they entered the breach.

Intellectuals and writers outside of the Soviet Union must continue to protest every new injustice there, for it is an imperative of conscience to do so and can mitigate, to some degree, the bitter fate of those who dare to oppose the Soviet authorities. But it would be in itself insufficient unless the example of the Soviet dissidents helps us strengthen our faith in those human values which are all that stand between us and final despair. There is as much to be learned from the drama of solitude and courage surrounding the writings of Sinyavsky's works as there is to be learned from those works themselves.

Notes

All the works of Tertz, except *Mysli vrasplokh* (*Thought Unaware*) and "Pkhentz," are published in *Fantasticheskiy mir Abrama Tertsa* (New York: Inter-Language Literary Associates, 1967). A reference to a page in this volume is given in parentheses at the end of a note. References to other Russian works for which English translations are cited are listed in the same manner.

Chapter 1. The Metamorphosis of Sinyavsky-Tertz

1. Leopold Labedz and Max Hayward, eds. *On Trial: The Case of Sinyavsky (Tertz) and Daniel (Arzhak)*, (London: Collins & Harvill, 1967), p. 333. There is also an American edition: Max Hayward, *On Trial: The Soviet State versus "Abram Tertz" and "Nikolai Arzhak"* (New York: Harper & Row, 1966), but the British edition contains much more information, including reminiscences of Sinyavsky as well as photographs taken by and of him, and is in every way more valuable. The minutes of the trial in Russian may be found in *Sinyavsky i Daniel' na skam'e podsudimykh*, intro. Hélène Zamoyska and Boris Filippov (New York: Inter-Language Literary Associates, 1966) as well as in Alexander Ginzburg, compiler, *Belaya kniga po delu A. Sinyavskogo i Yu. Danielya* (Frankfurt on the Main: Posev, 1967).

2. Svetlana Alliluyeva, *Only One Year* (New York: Harper & Row, 1969).

3. Labedz, Hayward, *On Trial*, p. 345.

4. *Ibid.*, p. 326.

5. *Ibid.,* p. 52.

6. *Ibid.,* p. 336.

7. Nikolai Berdyaev, *Dostoevsky,* trans. Donald Attwater (New York: World Pub., Meridian Books, 1957), p. i.

8. Labedz, Hayward, *On Trial,* p. 156.

9. *Ibid.,* pp. 48–49.

10. *Ibid.,* p. 49.

11. *Ibid.,* p. 340.

12. *Ibid.,* p. 191.

13. Abram Tertz, *The Trial Begins,* trans. Max Hayward (New York: Pantheon, 1960), p. 59 (233).

14. Labedz, Hayward, *On Trial,* p. 56. "Shame"—thus, responsibility.

15. *Ibid.,* p. 19. Original in *Tribune de Peuple,* Feb. 8, 1966.

16. Abram Tertz, *On Socialist Realism,* trans. George Dennis, intro. Czesław Miłosz (New York: Pantheon, 1960), p. 11.

17. The picture is, of course, more complex than I make it here, and the question of Pasternak is treated with more detail in Chapter 8. Akhmatova too was a link to the twenties, a poet of great stature, and one to whom many young poets, including Joseph Brodsky, turned for judgment and encouragement. But Pasternak had more influence on Sinyavsky.

18. Labedz, Hayward, *On Trial,* p. 60.

19. *Ibid.,* p. 61.

20. *Ibid.,* p. 61.

21. Andrei Sinyavsky, *For Freedom of Imagination,* ed., trans., and intro. Laszlo Tikos and Murray Peppard (New York: Holt, Rinehart & Winston, 1971), p. 135 (36).

22. Tertz, *The Trial Begins,* pp. 122–123 (272).

23. *Ibid.,* p. 122 (272).

24. *Sinyavsky i Daniel' na skam'e podsudimykh,* intro. Zamoyska and Filippov, p. 10. Zamoyska's article originally appeared in *Le Monde,* Feb. 16, 1966.

Chapter 2. The Trial

1. Alexander Ginzburg compiled the minutes of the Sinyavsky–Daniel trial (*Belaya kniga po delu A. Sinyavskogo i Yu. Danielya*),

but whether he personally took the notes at the trial is not known. The former editor of *Sintaksis*, a *samizdat* poetry journal, Ginzburg is a leading figure in the dissident movement and has been arrested several times.

2. Labedz, Hayward, *On Trial* (see note 1, Chapter 1).

3. *Ibid.*, pp. 91–92.

4. *Ibid.*, p. 95.

5. *Ibid.*, p. 95.

6. *Ibid.*

7. *Ibid.*, p. 36.

8. "Amalrik's Trial," *Russian Review*, Oct. 1971.

9. Labedz, Hayward, *On Trial*, p. 260.

10. *Ibid.*, p. 352. (Originally published in *L'Humanité*, Feb. 16, 1966.)

11. *Ibid.*, p. 289.

12. *Ibid.*, p. 291.

13. *Ibid.*, p. 41. (Originally published in *Pravda*, April 2, 1966.)

14. The comparison belongs to Labedz.

15. Quoted from the unpublished memoirs of Aleksander Wat by Czesław Miłosz in his article "On Modern Russian Literature and the West," *California Slavic Studies* (Berkeley: University of California Press, 1971), 174.

Chapter 3. On Socialist Realism

1. Mihajlo Mihajlov, *Russian Themes*, trans. Marija Mihajlov (New York: Farrar, Straus & Giroux, 1968), p. 4. (*Abram Tertz ili begstvo iz retorty* [Frankfurt on the Main: 1969], p. 5.)

2. Tertz, *On Socialist Realism*, trans. George Dennis (New York: Pantheon, 1960).

3. The guessing went on in the USSR as well. Boris Ryurikov concluded that Tertz was an émigré (*Inostrannaya literature*, no. 1, 1962).

4. Tertz, *On Socialist Realism*, intro. Miłosz, p. 7.

5. Tertz, *On Socialist Realism*, p. 26 (403).

6. Alexander Solzhenitsyn, *The First Circle*, trans. Thomas P. Whitney (New York: Harper & Row, 1968), p. 99. (*V kruge pervom* [New York: Harper Colophon Books, 1969], p. 90.)

204   Notes

7. Tertz, *On Socialist Realism*, p. 31 (406).
8. *Ibid.*, p. 32 (407).
9. *Ibid.*, p. 59 (424).
10. *Ibid.*, p. 41 (413).
11. *Ibid.*, p. 38 (411). Arthur Koestler, in the fourth volume of his autobiography, *The Invisible Writing* (Boston: Beacon Press, 1954), quotes from his own novel, *The Gladiators*, which he wrote when still a member of the Communist party in order to work out his mounting doubts. The following passage shows an uncanny similarity to Sinyavsky, a similarity which is the result of a literary imagination coming to terms with dialectical habits of mind. Spartacus is a victim of the "law of detours" which compels the leader on the road to Utopia to be "ruthless for the sake of pity." He is "doomed always to do that which is most repugnant to him, to become a slaughterer in order to abolish slaughter, to whip people with knouts so that they may learn not to let themselves be whipped, to strip himself of every scruple in the name of a higher scrupulousness" pp. 267–268.

12. Isaac Deutscher, *The Unfinished Revolution, Russia 1917–1967* (New York: Oxford University Press, 1967), p. 37. To speak of the tragedy of Soviet communism in terms of a means-ends confusion has become somewhat standard, for good and obvious reasons. Koestler, for example, writes in *Arrow in the Blue* (New York: Macmillan, 1961): "At least during the initial stages of their Party career, the Promethean vision dominated the destructive tendency. In later years I saw them change one by one, as the End received from their vision, and the Means alone remained" p. 280.

13. Stefan Bergholz (pseudonym of Aleksander Wat), "On Reading Tertz," Survey, no. 41, April, 1962. This is a small segment of a much larger study of Sinyavsky, "Czytając Terca," which appeared as the introduction to the Polish (émigré) translation of *Fantasticheskie rasskazy—Opowieści Fantastyczne*, trans. Jozef Lobodowski and Stefan Bergholz (Paris: Instytut Literacki, 1961).

14. This translation, mine of Wat's "Łucznistwo Japońskie" was first published in *Stony Brook* (New York: Stony Brook Poetics

Foundation, Fall 1968), p. 118. The original may be found in Aleksander Wat, *Ciemne Świecidło* (Paris: Libella, 1968), p. 135.

15. Tertz, *On Socialist Realism*, p. 57 (432).

16. *Ibid.*, pp. 74–75 (433).

17. *Ibid.*, p. 80 (437).

18. *Ibid.*, pp. 65–66 (428).

19. Andrei Amalrik, *Will the Soviet Union Survive until 1984?* (New York: Harper & Row, Perennial Library, 1971), p. 101.

20. Tertz, *On Socialist Realism*, p. 89 (442).

21. *Ibid.*, p. 93 (445).

22. *Ibid.*, p. 92 (444).

23. Labedz, Hayward, *On Trial*, p. 336.

24. Tertz, *On Socialist Realism*, p. 89 (442)

25. *Ibid.*, p. 90 (443–444).

26. *Ibid.*, pp. 94–95 (446).

27. Amalrik, *Will the Soviet Union Survive until 1984?*, p. 6.

Chapter 4. The Trial Begins

1. Georg Lukács, *The Historical Novel*, trans. Hannah and Stanley Mitchell (London: Merlin Press, 1962).

2. Georg von Rauch, *A History of Soviet Russia*, 5th rev. ed., trans. Peter and Annette Jacobsohn (New York: Praeger, 1967).

3. Andrei Amalrik, *Involuntary Journey to Siberia*, trans. Manya Harari and Max Hayward (New York: Harcourt Brace Jovanovich, 1970), p. 171.

4. The theme of the crisis of the thirtieth years can also be found in Witold Gombrowicz's novel *Ferdydurke*. A psychological investigation of this theme is to be found in Erich Fromm's *The Forgotten Language*.

5. Solzhenitsyn, *The First Circle*, p. 116 (106).

6. Tertz, *The Trial Begins*, p. 91 (253).

7. *Ibid.*, p. 24 (210).

8. *Ibid.*, p. 25 (210).

9. *Ibid.*, p. 62 (234).

10. *Ibid.*, p. 45 (223).

11. *Ibid.*, p. 79 (246).

12. Amalrik, *Will the Soviet Union Survive until 1984?* p. 96.

13. Tertz, *The Trial Begins,* pp. 38–39 (219).

14. See Tertz, *On Socialist Realism,* pp. 57–64 (425–429) for Sinyavsky's remarks on political and erotic symbols in Russian literature.

15. Tertz, *The Trial Begins,* pp. 48–49 (224).

16. *Ibid.,* p. 87 (251).

17. *Ibid.,* p. 74 (242).

18. *Ibid.,* p. 59 (233).

19. *Ibid.,* pp. 115–116 (268).

20. Amalrik, *Will the Soviet Union Survive until 1984?,* p. 34.

21. Leonid Rzhevsky, "The New Idiom," in *Soviet Literature in the Sixties,* ed. Max Hayward, Edward L. Crowley (New York: Praeger, 1964), p. 65.

Chapter 5. Solitaria

1. Labedz, Hayward, *On Trial,* p. 196.

2. Stanisław Lec, *Unkempt Thoughts,* trans. Jacek Galazka (New York: Minerva Press, 1962), pp. 55, 78, 61.

3. V. V. Rozanov, *Solitaria,* trans. S. S. Koteliansky (New York: Boni and Liveright, 1927). p. 47 (*Uedinennoe* [Petrograd: "Novoe vremya," 1916], p. 1).

4. Abram Tertz, *Mysli vrasplokh,* intro. Andrew Field (New York: Rausen, 1966), p. 45. This aphorism and those referred to in notes 5, 8–14, 16–17, 19–21, and 23–36 can be found in a translation of *Mysli vrasplokh* by Robert Szulkin and Andrew Field, "Thought Unaware," *New Leader,* July 19, 1965, on pages 16–26. In a few instances I have retranslated when I considered it necessary. This is very similar to Rozanov's: "I may be a 'fool' (there are rumours), perhaps even a 'swindler' (there is gossip to that effect); but the *width* of thought, the *incommensurability* of 'horizons revealed'—no one has had that before me in the way I possess it. And all of it came from my own mind, without borrowing an iota even." V. V. Rozanov, *Solitaria,* trans. S. S. Koteliansky (London: Wishart, 1927), p. 116.

5. Tertz, *Mysli vrasplokh,* p. 147.

6. Bergholz, "On Reading Tertz," p. 145.

7. D. H. Lawrence, "A Review of *Solitaria*," in *Phoenix, The Posthumous Papers of D. H. Lawrence*, ed. Edward McDonald (London: William Heineman, 1961), p. 371.

8. Tertz, *Mysli vrasplokh*, p. 33.

9. *Ibid.*, p. 64.

10. *Ibid.*, p. 66.

11. *Ibid.*, p. 55.

12. *Ibid.*, p. 43.

13. *Ibid.*, p. 58.

14. *Ibid.*, p. 94.

15. Rozanov, *Solitaria*, p. 90 (74).

16. Tertz, *Mysli vrasplokh*, p. 72.

17. *Ibid.*, p. 46.

18. Yevgeny Vinokurov, *Muzyka* (Moscow: Sovetskiy Pisatel', 1964). Trans. by author.

19. V. V. Rozanov, *Opavshie list'ya* (Berlin: Rossica, 1929), p. 250. Trans. by author.

20. Tertz, *Mysli vrasplokh*, p. 49.

21. *Ibid.*, p. 49.

22. Carl Jung, "The Soul and Death," *Collected Works* (New York: Bollingen, 1953), vol. 8, p. 218.

23. Tertz, *Mysli vrasplokh*, p. 108.

24. *Ibid.*, p. 100.

25. *Ibid.*, p. 87.

26. *Ibid.*, p. 110.

27. *Ibid.*, p. 124.

28. *Ibid.*, p. 56.

29. *Ibid.*, p. 122.

30. *Ibid.*, p. 80.

31. *Ibid.*, p. 80.

32. *Ibid.*, p. 92.

33. *Ibid.*, p. 84.

34. *Ibid.*, p. 137.

35. *Ibid.*, p. 139.

36. *Ibid.*, p. 69.

Chapter 6. Science and Fiction: *Fantastic Stories*

1. Mihalov, *Russian Themes*, p. 39 (*Abram Terts ili begstvo iz retorty*, p. 45).

2. *Ibid.*, p. 72 (79).

3. Fyodor Dostoevsky, *The Best Short Stories of Dostoevsky*, trans., intro. David Magarshack (New York: Modern Library, undated), p. 318 (*Son smeshnogo cheloveka, Dnevnik pisatelya za 1877 god* [Paris: YMCA Press], p. 158).

4. Abram Tertz, *Fantastic Stories*, trans. Max Hayward and Ronald Hingley (New York: Pantheon, 1963), p. 148 (27).

5. *Ibid.*, p. 158 (34).

6. *Ibid.*, p. 155 (33).

7. *Ibid.*, p. 154 (31–32).

8. *Ibid.*, p. 160 (36).

9. For a good treatment of this subject see Aleksander Hertz, *Żydzi w kulturze polskiej* (Paris: Instytut Literacki, 1961).

10. Nadezhda Mandelstam, *Hope against Hope*, trans. Max Hayward (New York: Atheneum, 1970), p. 88, p. 297.

11. Tertz, *Fantastic Stories*, p. 3 (42).

12. *Ibid.*, p. 22 (56).

13. *Ibid.*, p. 14 (50).

14. *Ibid.*, p. 130 (67–68).

15. Carl Jung, *The Integration of the Personality*, trans. Stanley M. Dell (New York: Farrar and Rinehart, 1939), p. 72.

16. Tertz, *Fantastic Stories*, p. 188 (89).

17. *Ibid.*, pp. 195–196 (94–95).

18. *Ibid.*, p. 210 (104–105).

19. *Ibid.*, p. 65 (130).

20. *Ibid.*, p. 95 (154).

21. *Ibid.*, pp. 80, 83 (142, 144).

22. *Ibid.*, p. 35 (108).

23. *Ibid.*, p. 116 (170).

24. Abram Tertz, "Pkhentz" in *Soviet Short Stories*, vol. 2, ed. Peter Reddaway, trans. Jeremy Biddulph (Baltimore: Penguin, 1968), p. 219.

25. *Ibid.*, p. 225.
26. *Ibid.*, p. 241.

Chapter 7. History versus the People

1. Abram Tertz, *The Makepeace Experiment*, trans. Manya Harari (New York: Random House, 1965), p. 49 (301).
2. *Ibid.*, p. 137 (359).
3. *Ibid.*, p. 30 (288).
4. "Rusi yest' veseliye piti, ne mozhet bez togo byti"—quoted by Dmitrii Cizevskii in his *History of Russian Literature from the Eleventh Century to the End of the Baroque* (The Hague: Mouton, 1962), p. 13.
5. Tertz, *The Makepeace Experiment*, p. 75 (318–319).
6. Labedz, Hayward, *On Trial*, p. 197.
7. This translation is based on the prose translation which appears in *Penguin Book of Russian Verse*, intro., ed. Dimitri Obolensky (Baltimore: Penguin Books, 1962), p. 138.
8. Tertz, *The Makepeace Experiment*, p. 85 (325–326).
9. *Ibid.*, p. 85 (326).
10. Labedz, Hayward, *On Trial*, p. 343.
11. Gregory Pomerants, "Man without an Adjective," trans. and abr. Alexis Koriakov, *Russian Review*, July 1971, pp. 219–220.
12. Tertz, *The Makepeace Experiment*, p. 58 (308).
13. *Bitter Harvest*, ed. Edmund Stillman (New York: Praeger, 1959), "Poem for Adults" by Adam Ważyk, pp. 129–136; permission of *East Europe*. Originally published in *Nowa Kultura* (Warsaw), Sept. 21, 1955, as "Poemat dla doroslych."
14. Tertz, *The Makepeace Experiment*, pp. 176–177 (386).
15. Amalrik, *Will the Soviet Union Survive until 1984?*, p. 67.

Chapter 8. Sinyavsky as a Critic

1. Labedz, Hayward, *On Trial*, p. 217.
2. Andrei Sinyavsky, *For Freedom of Imagination*, p. vii.
3. These twenty pieces of criticism are listed in full in the bibliography.
4. A. D. Sinyavsky, "A. M. Gorkiy," in *Istoriya russkoy sovet-*

210 Notes

skoy literatury, I (Moscow: Izdatel'stvo akademii nauk SSSR, 1958), 99. Trans. by author.

5. Georg Lukács, *Studies in European Realism* (New York: Grosset and Dunlap, 1964), p. 206.

6. Tertz, *On Socialist Realism*, p. 68 (430).

7. A. D. Sinyavsky, "Literatura perioda velikoy otechestvennoy voyny," in *Istoriya russkoy sovetskoy literatury*, 3 (Moscow: Izdatel'stvo akedemii nauk SSSR, 1961), 28. Trans. by author.

8. A. D. Sinyavsky, "Eduard Bagritskiy," in *Istoriya russkoy sovetskoy literatury*, 1 (Moscow: Izdatel'stvo akaemii nauk SSSR, 1958), 399. Trans. by author.

9. A. Menshutin, A. Sinyavsky, "Den' russkoy poezii," *Novy mir*, no. 2, Feb. 1959, p. 216. Trans. by author.

10. A. Menshutin, A. Sinyavsky, "Davayte govorit' professional'no," *Novy mir*, no. 8, Aug. 1961, p. 251. Trans. by author. The six articles which attacked Sinyavsky and Menshutin's "Den' russkoy poezii" and to which they are here responding are as follows:

1. V. Busin, "Fialki pakhnut ne tem," *Literatura i zhizn'*, Feb. 17, 1961.

2. D. Starikov, "Sporit' po sushchestvu!" *Literatura i zhizn'*, Feb. 24, 1961.

3. S. Smirnov, "Metnulo! Replika dvum kritikam," *Ogonek*, no. 9, 1961.

4. K. Lisovskiy, "Kuda-to ne tuda . . . Zametki o 'sibirskikh' stikhakh A. Voznesenskogo," *Sibirskie ogni*, no. 4, 1961.

5. V. Federov, "Vesennyaya vstrecha," *Molodaya gvardiya*, no. 5, 1961.

6. B. Solov'ev, "Legkiy nesesser i tyazhelaja klad'," *Oktyabr'*, no. 6, 1961.

11. Sinyavsky, *For Freedom of Imagination*, p. 169 (116).

12-15. Andrei Sinyavsky, "Isaac Babel" in *Major Soviet Writers, Essays in Criticism*, Edward J. Brown, ed. (New York: Oxford University Press, 1973), pp. 301-307. The translation by Catherine Brown differs from mine.

16. Aldous Huxley, *The Doors of Perception* and *Heaven and Hell* (London: Penguin, 1961), p. 15.

17. I. Golomshtok, A. Sinyavsky, *Pikasso,* (Moscow: Znanie, 1960), p. 17. Trans. by author.

18. *Ibid.,* p. 33.

19. Sinyavsky. *For Freedom of Imagination,* p. 110 (15).

20. *Ibid.,* p. 104 (10).

21. Czesław Miłosz, "On Pasternak Soberly," *Books Abroad,* Spring 1970, p. 207.

22. Sinyavsky, *For Freedom of Imagination,* p. 111 (16).

23. *Ibid.,* p. 113 (17).

24. Nadezhda Mandelstam, *Hope against Hope,* p. 150.

25. A. Menshutin, A. Sinyavsky, *Poeziya pervykh let revolutsii 1917–1920,* (Moscow: "Nauka," 1961), p. 150. Trans. by author.

26. Leonid Vladimirov (pseud. of Leonid Vladimirovich Finkel'-steyn), *Rossiya bez prikras i umolchaniy* (Frankfurt on the Main: Posev, 1969), pp. 296–297. Nadezhda Mandelstam also takes a less "romantic" view of the twenties. In *Hope against Hope* she writes: "This hankering after the idyllic twenties is the result of a legend created by people who were then in their thirties, and by younger associates. But in reality it was the twenties in which all the foundations were laid for the future: the casuistical dialectic, the dismissal of older values, the longing for unanimity and self-abasement" p. 168.

27. Cf. Tertz, *On Socialist Realism,* pp. 80–81 (437).

28. Menshutin, Sinyavsky, *Poeziya pervykh let revolutsii 1917–1920,* p. 354. Trans. by author.

29. *Ibid.,* p. 146.

30. *Ibid.,* p. 138.

31. *Ibid.,* p. 136.

32. *Ibid.,* p. 340.

33. *Ibid.,* p. 257.

34. *Ibid.,* pp. 261–262.

35. Boris Pasternak, *An Essay in Autobiography,* trans. Manya Harari (London: Collins and Harvill, 1959), p. 103.

36. Menshutin, Sinyavsky, *Poeziya pervykh let revolutsii,* p. 274. Trans. by author.

37. Labedz, Hayward, *On Trial,* p. 210.

Selected Bibliography

Allilueva, Svetlana. *Only One Year*. New York: Harper & Row. 1969.

Amalrik, Andrei. *Involuntary Journey to Siberia*. Translated by Manya Harari and Max Hayward. New York: Harcourt Brace Jovanovich, 1970.

——. *Will the Soviet Union Survive until 1984?* New York: Harper & Row, 1971.

"Amalrik's Trial." *Russian Review*, vol. 30, no. 4 (Oct. 1971).

Arzhak, Nikolai. See Daniel, Yuliy.

Berdyaev, Nikolai. *Mirosozertsanie Dostoevskogo*. Prague: YMCA Press, 1923. (*Dostoevsky*. Translated by Donald Attwater. New York: World Pub., Meridian Books, 1957.)

——. *O rabstve i svobode cheloveka*. Paris: YMCA Press, 194–? (*Slavery and Freedom*. Translated by R. M. French. New York: Scribner's, 1944.)

Bergholz, Stefan. See Wat, Aleksander.

Brown, Deming. "The Art of Andrei Sinyavsky." *Slavic Review*, Dec. 1970.

Daniel, Yuliy [Nikolai Arzhak]. *Govorit Moskva*. New York: Inter-Language Literary Associates, 1966. (Translated as "This Is Moscow Speaking," in *Dissonant Voices in Soviet Literature*. Edited by Patricia Blake and Max Hayward. New York: Pantheon, 1962.)

Deutscher, Isaac. *The Unfinished Revolution, Russia 1917–1967*. New York: Oxford University Press, 1967.

Dostoevsky, Fyodor. "Son smeshnogo cheloveka." In *Dnevnik pisatelya za 1877 god*. Paris: YMCA Press. ("The Dream of a Ridiculous Man." In *The Best Short Stories of Dostoevsky*.

Translation and introduction by David Magarshack. New York: Modern Library.)

Field, Andrew. "Abram Tertz's Ordeal by Mirror." Introduction to Abram Tertz, *Mysli vrasplokh.* New York: Rausen, 1966.

Finkelshtayn, Leonid [Vladimirov, Leonid]. *Rossiya bez prikras i umolchaniy.* Frankfurt: Posev, 1969. (*The Russians.* New York: Praeger, 1968.)

Ginzburg, Alexander, compiler. *Belaya kniga po delu A. Sinyavskogo i Yu. Danielya.* Frankfurt: Posev, 1967.

Hertz, Aleksander. *Żydzi w kulturze Polskiej.* Paris: Instytut Literacki, 1961.

Huxley, Aldous. *The Doors of Perception* and *Heaven and Hell.* London: Penguin, 1961.

Jung, Carl. *The Integration of the Personality.* New York: Farrar and Rinehart, 1939.

——. "The Soul and Death." *Collected Works of Carl Jung.* New York: Bollingen, 1953.

Kedrina, Z. "Nasledniki Smerdyakova" ("The Heirs of Smerdyakov"). *Literaturnaya gazeta,* Jan. 22, 1966.

Koestler, Arthur. *Arrow in the Blue.* New York: Macmillan, 1961.

——. *The Invisible Writing.* Boston: Beacon Press, 1954.

Kołakowski, Leszek. "What Is Socialism?" *Bitter Harvest.* Edited by Edmund Stillman and François Bundy. New York: Praeger, 1959.

Labedz, Leopold, and Hayward, Max, eds. *On Trial: The Case of Sinyavsky (Tertz) and Daniel (Arzhak).* London: Collins & Harvill, 1967.

Lawrence, D. H. "A Review of Solitaria." *Phoenix: The Posthumous Papers of D. H. Lawrence.* Edited by Edward McDonald. London: William Heineman, 1961.

Lec, Stanisław. *Unkempt Thoughts.* Translated by Jacek Galazka. New York: Minerva Press, 1962.

Lukács, Georg. *The Historical Novel.* London: Merlin Press, 1962.

——. *Studies in European Realism.* New York: Grosset & Dunlap, 1964.

Mandelstam, Nadezhda. *Hope against Hope.* Translated by Max Hayward. New York: Atheneum, 1970.

Medvedev, Zhores A., and Roy A. *A Question of Madness.* Translated by Ellen de Kadt. New York: Knopf, 1971.

Mihajlov, Mihajlo. *Abram Terts ili begstvo iz retorty.* Frankfurt: Posev, 1969. (Appears under the title "Flight from the Test Tube," in *Russian Themes.* Translated by Marija Mihajlov. New York: Farrar, Straus & Giroux, 1968.)

Miłosz, Czesław. "On Pasternak Soberly." *Books Abroad,* vol. 44, no. 2 (Spring 1970).

———. Introduction to Abram Tertz, *On Socialist Realism.* New York: Pantheon, 1958.

Pasternak, Boris. *Doctor Zhivago.* Translated by Max Hayward and Manya Harari. New York: Pantheon, 1958.

———. *An Essay in Autobiography.* Translated by Manya Harari. London: Collins and Harvill, 1959.

———. *Stikhotvoreniya i poemy.* Moscow-Leningrad: Sovetskiy pisatel', 1961.

———. *Stikhotvoreniya i poemy.* Moscow-Leningrad: Sovetskiy pisatel', 1965.

Pomerants, Gregory. "Man without an Adjective." *Russian Review,* vol. 30, no. 3 (July 1971).

Rozanov, V. V. *Opavshie list'ya.* Berlin: Rossica, 1929.

———. *Solitaria.* Translated by S. S. Koteliansky. London: Wishart, 1927.

———. *Uedinennoe.* Petrograd: Novoe vremya, 1916.

Rzhevsky, Leonid. "The New Idiom." *Soviet Literature in the Sixties.* Edited by Max Hayward and Edward L. Crowley. New York: Praeger, 1964.

Sinyavsky and Daniel' na skam'e podsudimykh. Introduction by Hélène Zamoyska and Boris Filippov. New York: Inter-Language Literary Associates, 1966.

Sinyavsky, Andrei. "A. M. Gorkiy." *Istoriya russkoy sovetskoy literatury.* Vol. 1. Moscow: Academy of Sciences USSR, 1958.

———. "Bez skidok." *Voprosy literatury,* no. 1, 1960. (Translated as "No Discount," in *For Freedom of Imagination.* See below.)

———. "Boris Pasternak." *Pasternak, Modern Judgements.* Edited by Donald Davie and Angela Livingstone. London: Macmillan, 1969.

——. "Eduard Bagritskiy." *Istoriya russkoy sovetskoy literatury.* Vol. 1. Moscow: Academy of Sciences USSR, 1958.

——. "Est' takie stikhi." *Novy mir,* no. 3, 1965. (Translated as "There Are Such Verses," in *For Freedom of Imagination.*)

——. *For Freedom of Imagination.* Translation and introduction by Laszlo Tikos and Murray Peppard. New York: Holt, Rinehart & Winston, 1971.

——. Introduction to Boris Pasternak, *Stikhotvoreniya i poemy.* Moscow-Leningrad: Sovetskiy pisatel', 1965. (Translations appear in *Pasternak, Modern Judgements,* and *For Freedom of Imagination.*)

——. "Isaac Babel."*Oeuvres et Opinions,* no. 8, 1964. (Translation in *Major Soviet Writers, Essays in Criticism.* Edward J. Brown. New York: Oxford University Press, 1973.)

——. "Literatura perioda velikoy otechestvennoy voyny." *Istoriya russkoy sovetskoy literatury.* Vol. 3. Moscow: Academy of Sciences USSR, 1961.

——. "O novom sbornike stikhov Anatolya Sofronova." *Novy mir,* no. 8. 1959. (Translated as "On a Collection of Verses by Anatoly Sofronov," in *For Freedom of Imagination.*)

——. "Pamflet ili paskvil?" *Novy mir,* no. 12, 1964. (Translated as "Pamphlet or Lampoon?" in *For Freedom of Imagination.*)

——. "Poeticheskiy sbornik B. Pasternak." *Novy mir,* no. 3, 1962.

——. "Poeziya i proza Ol'gi Berggolts." *Novy mir,* no. 5, 1960. (Translated as "The Poetry and Prose of Olga Berggolts" in *For Freedom of Imagination.*)

——. "Poydem so mnoy . . ." *Novy mir,* no. 1, 1964. (Translated as "Come Walk with Us" in *For Freedom of Imagination.*)

——. "Raskovanniy golos." *Novy mir,* no. 6, 1964. (Translated as "The Unfettered Voice" in *For Freedom of Imagination.*)

——. "Realizm fantastiki." *Literaturnaya gazeta,* no. 1 (May 1960).

——. "V zashchitu piramidy, zametki o tvorchestve Yevg. Yevtushenko i ego poeme 'Bratskaya GES.'" *Grani,* no. 63, 1967. (Translated as "In Defense of the Pyramid" in *For Freedom of Imagination.*)

——, and I. Golomshtok. *Pikasso.* Moscow: Znanie, 1960.

——, and A. Men'shutin. "Davayte govorit' profesional'no." *Novy mir*, no. 8, 1961.

——, and A. Men'shutin. "Den' russkoy poezii." *Novy mir*, no. 2, 1959.

——, and A. Men'shutin. *Poeziya pervykh let revolutsii, 1917–1920.* Moscow: "Nauka," 1964.

——, and A. Men'shutin. "Za poeticheskuyu aktivnost'." *Novy mir*, no. 1, 1961.

—— [Abram Tertz]. *Fantasticheskiy mir Abram Tertz.* New York: Inter-Language Literary Associates, 1967.

——. *Fantastic Stories.* Translated by Max Hayward and Ronald Hingley. New York: Random House, 1963.

——. *The Makepeace Experiment.* Translated by Manya Harari. New York: Random House, 1965.

——. *Mysli vrasplokh.* New York: Rausen, 1966. (Translated by Andrew Field and Robert Szulkin as *Thought Unaware.* Appeared in *The New Leader,* vol. 48, no. 15 [July 19, 1965].)

——. *On Socialist Realism.* Translated by George Dennis. New York: Pantheon, 1960.

——. "Pkhentz." In *Soviet Short Stories.* Vol. 2. Edited by Peter Reddaway. Baltimore: Penguin, 1968. (Bilingual edition, contains original and translation.)

——. *The Trial Begins.* Translated by Max Hayward. New York: Pantheon, 1960.

Solzhenitsyn, Alexander. *One Day in the Life of Ivan Denisovich.* New York: Praeger, 1963.

——. *V kruge pervom.* New York: Harper Colophon Books, 1969. Russian edition also published by YMCA Press, Paris, 1969. (*The First Circle.* Translated by Thomas P. Whitney. New York: Harper & Row, 1968.)

Tertz, Abram. See Sinyavsky, Andrei.

Trotsky, Leon. *Literature and Revolution.* Ann Arbor: University of Michigan Press, 1960.

Vinokurov, Yevgeniy. *Muzyka.* Moscow: Sovetskiy pisatel', 1964.

Vladimirov, Leonid. See Finkel'shtayn, Leonid. *Rossiya bez prikras i umolchaniy.* Frankfurt: Posev, 1969. (*The Russians.* New York: Praeger, 1968.)

Von Rauch, Georg. *A History of Soviet Russia.* 5th rev. ed. New York: Praeger, 1967.

Wat, Aleksander. "Japanese Archery." *Stony Brook,* vol. 1/2 (Fall 1968).

——. From Wat's as yet unpublished memoirs. Quoted by Czesław Miłosz in "On Modern Russian Literature and the West." *California Slavic Studies,* vol. 6. Berkeley: University of California Press, 1971.

—— [Stefan Bergholz]. "Czytając Terca." Introduction to Abram Tertz, *Opowieści fantastyczne.* Paris: Instytut Literacki, 1961. (Partial translation published under pseudonym Stefan Bergholz. "On Reading Tertz," *Survey,* no. 41, April 1962.)

Ważyk, Adam. "Poem for Adults." *Bitter Harvest.* Edited by Edmund Stillman and François Bundy. New York: Praeger, 1959.

Yeremin, Dmitri. "Perevertyshi" ("The Turncoats"). *Izvestiya,* Jan. 13, 1966.

Index

Letters to the Future

Designed by R. E. Rosenbaum.
Composed by Vail-Ballou Press, Inc.,
in 11 point linotype Janson, 3 points leaded,
with display lines in monotype Janson.
Printed letterpress from type by Vail-Ballou Press
on Warren's No. 66 Text, 60 lb. basis,
with the Cornell University Press watermark.
Bound by Vail-Ballou Press
in Columbia Bayside Vellum
and stamped in All Purpose foil.

Letters to the Future

An Approach to Sinyavsky-Tertz

Richard Lourie

To fill the void that resulted from the
shattering of his Marxist beliefs, Andrei
Sinyavsky invented Abram Tertz.
Weaving together biography and keen
literary insights, this book traces the
metamorphosis of Sinyavsky, teacher
and critic, into Tertz, clandestine
writer of fantastical fiction. It reviews
the crises in Soviet society before and
after Stalin's death, and describes the
loss of faith that precipitated
Sinyavsky's dual existence, ending
with the writer's arrest, trial, and
imprisonment in 1966.

Sympathetic yet critical, Mr. Lourie
treats all of Sinyavsky's pretrial
writings. He discusses **The Trial Begins,
Thought Unaware, On Socialist
Realism, Fantastic Stories,** and
The Makepeace Experiment as works
of art and as visible signs of complex
and changing relationships. Each work
is assessed in the context within which
it was written, and is compared with
other Russian works and with contemporary Polish, European, and American
writings. Sinyavsky's literary criticism,
published in Russia under his own
name, is evaluated on its own terms and
in the light of his fiction.

In addition to all of the published
writings, Mr. Lourie makes full use
of the record of Sinyavsky's trial,
reminiscences of his friends, and the
small body of critical literature
available. The book provides not only